SOLILOQUIES,
& SONGS
From the Plays

SPEECHES, SOLILOQUIES, & SONGS
From the Plays

William Shakespeare

Edited,
with an introduction,
by David Alexander

RUNNING BROOK PRESS

Published by
Running Brook Press
Denver, Colorado 80212
USA

ISBN 978-0-9910119-0-2

Library of Congress Control Number:
2013951488

TABLE OF CONTENTS

INTRODUCTION

This book attempts to bring together in one place
the most famous speeches, soliloquies, and songs
from the plays of Shakespeare. To some, removing
these passages from the plays and placing them in
isolation would only obscure their dramatic context
and thereby diminish their meaning and power. It
is true that for many of the passages, knowing the
details of a given scene or play can only deepen
one's appreciation of the text. In one of the most
famous passages in Shakespeare, Macbeth's nihilis-
tic meditation on the incessant cruelty of time and
the apparent meaninglessness of action, in which
he begins "Tomorrow, and tomorrow, and tomorrow / Creeps in this petty pace from day to day,"
we cannot fully appreciate his state of mind without
knowing he has just learned that his wife has killed
herself, and that meanwhile the armies of Malcolm
and Macduff have begun gradually surrounding his
castle, closing off any possible escape.

Still, these passages continue to speak to us so
strongly because they so easily live beyond the
plays that contain them—they shed light on universal truths greater than the specific issues at stake
in Macbeth's Scotland, or Hamlet's Denmark, or
Brutus' Rome. At their core the plays of Shakespeare
are *poetry*, and the essential passages from the plays
form perhaps the most important and influential
body of poetic work in all of English literature, if
not in all world literature.

The speeches and soliloquies included here were chosen primarily for their importance and popularity among a wide range of audiences. A number of them will be familiar to all readers as those most often taught in school; others have been selected based on their special importance to actors and scholars for representing key moments in the dramatic action; still others have been included for the sheer power and beauty of their words, many of which form a kind of cultural foundation that informs much of how we think and act in the modern world; a few are simply my personal favorites. Shakespeare's vocal songs are often underappreciated in collections such as this one, and of the seventy or so songs in the plays, I have included twelve of the best here. Ultimately, my hope is that this collection will be both a convenient resource for the discovery of some of the most important passages from Shakespeare's plays as well as a stepping stone for the reader to seek out more from the complete plays in print and in performance.

David Alexander

A NOTE ABOUT THE TEXTS

The texts used in this book are based primarily on the quarto and folio control texts recommended by Stanley Wells and Gary Taylor in *William Shakespeare: A Textual Companion*. All act and scene designations are based on *The Norton Shakespeare* edition, itself based on the *The Oxford Shakespeare* edition.

SPEECHES,
SOLILOQUIES,
& SONGS
From the Plays

ENOBARBUS
The barge she sat in, like a burnished throne,
Burned on the water. The poop was beaten gold.
Purple the sails, and so perfumèd that
The winds were love-sick with them. The oars were silver,
Which to the tune of flutes kept stroke, and made
The water which they beat to follow faster,
As amorous of their strokes. For her own person,
It beggared all description. She did lie
In her pavilion, cloth of gold, of tissue,
O'er-picturing that Venus where we see
The fancy outworked nature. On each side her
Stood pretty dimpled boys, like smiling Cupids,
With divers-coloured fans whose wind did seem
To glow the delicate cheeks which they did cool,
And what they undid did...
Her gentlewomen, like the Nereides,
So many mermaids, tended her i'th' eyes
And made their bends adornings. At the helm
A seeming mermaid steers. The silken tackle
Swell with the touches of those flower-soft hands
That yarely frame the office. From the barge
A strange invisible perfume hits the sense
Of the adjacent wharfs. The city cast
Her people out upon her, and Antony,
Enthroned i'th' marketplace, did sit alone,
Whistling to th'air, which but for vacancy
Had gone to gaze on Cleopatra too,
And made a gap in nature...
Upon her landing Antony sent to her,

Invited her to supper. She replied
It should be better he became her guest,
Which she entreated. Our courteous Antony,
Whom ne'er the word of 'No' woman heard speak,
Being barbered ten times o'er, goes to the feast,
And for his ordinary, pays his heart
For what his eyes eat only...
                              I saw her once
Hop forty paces through the public street,
And, having lost her breath, she spoke and panted,
That she did make defect perfection,
And breathless, pour breath forth...
Age cannot wither her, nor custom stale
Her infinite variety. Other women cloy
The appetites they feed, but she makes hungry
Where most she satisfies. For vilest things
Become themselves in her, that the holy priests
Bless her when she is riggish.

(Act 2, Scene 2)

CLEOPATRA
I dreamt there was an Emperor Antony.
O, such another sleep, that I might see
But such another man!...
His face was as the heav'ns, and therein stuck
A sun and moon which kept their course and lighted
The little O, th'earth...
His legs bestrid the ocean, his reared arm
Crested the world. His voice was propertied
As all the tunèd spheres, and that to friends.
But when he meant to quail and shake the orb,
He was as rattling thunder. For his bounty,
There was no winter in't. An autumn it was,
That grew the more by reaping. His delights
Were dolphin-like, they showed his back above
The element they lived in. In his livery
Walked crowns and crownets. Realms and islands were
As plates dropped from his pocket...
But if there be or ever were one such,
It's past the size of dreaming. Nature wants stuff
To vie strange forms with fancy, yet t'imagine
An Anthony were nature's piece 'gainst fancy,
Condemning shadows quite.

(Act 5, Scene 2)

DUKE SENIOR

Now, my co-mates and brothers in exile,
Hath not old custom made this life more sweet
Than that of painted pomp? Are not these woods
More free from peril than the envious court?
Here feel we not the penalty of Adam,
The seasons' difference, as the icy fang
And churlish chiding of the winter's wind
Which, when it bites and blows upon my body,
Even till I shrink with cold, I smile and say:
This is no flattery, these are counsellors
That feelingly persuade me what I am.
Sweet are the uses of adversity
Which, like the toad, ugly and venomous,
Wears yet a precious jewel in his head.
And this our life, exempt from public haunt,
Finds tongues in trees, books in the running brooks,
Sermons in stones, and good in everything.

(Act 2, Scene 1)

AMIENS
Under the greenwood tree,
    Who loves to lie with me,
And turn his merry note,
    Unto the sweet bird's throat,
Come hither, come hither, come hither.
    Here shall he see no enemy,
But winter and rough weather.

Who doth ambition shun,
    And loves to live i'th' sun,
Seeking the food he eats,
    And pleased with what he gets,
Come hither, come hither, come hither.
    Here shall he see no enemy,
But winter and rough weather.
                              (Act 2, Scene 5)

JAQUES
If it do come to pass,
    That any man turn ass,
Leaving his wealth and ease,
    A stubborn will to please,
Ducdame, ducdame, ducdame.
    Here shall he see gross fools as he,
And if he will come to me.

(Act 2, Scene 5)

JAQUES
A fool, a fool! I met a fool i'th' forest!
A motley fool, a miserable world.
As I do live by food, I met a fool
Who laid him down and basked him in the sun,
And railed on Lady Fortune in good terms,
In good set terms, and yet a motley fool.
'Good morrow, fool,' quoth I. 'No, sir,' quoth he,
'Call me not fool till heaven hath sent me fortune.'
And then he drew a dial from his poke,
And looking on it with lack-lustre eye
Says, very wisely, 'It is ten o'clock.
Thus we may see', quoth he, 'how the world wags.
'Tis but an hour ago since it was nine.
And after one hour more 'twill be eleven.
And so from hour to hour we ripe and ripe.
And then from hour to hour we rot and rot.
And thereby hangs a tale.' When I did hear
The motley fool thus moral on the time,
My lungs began to crow like chanticleer
That fools should be so deep contemplative.
And I did laugh, sans intermission,
An hour by his dial. O, noble fool,
A worthy fool! Motley's the only wear.
                                        (Act 2, Scene 7)

JAQUES

     All the world's a stage,
And all the men and women merely players.
They have their exits and their entrances,
And one man in his time plays many parts,
His acts being seven ages. At first, the infant,
Mewling and puking in the nurse's arms.
Then, the whining schoolboy with his satchel
And shining morning face, creeping like snail
Unwillingly to school. And then the lover,
Sighing like furnace, with a woeful ballad
Made to his mistress' eyebrow. Then a soldier,
Full of strange oaths and bearded like the pard,
Jealous in honour, sudden and quick in quarrel,
Seeking the bubble reputation
Even in the canon's mouth. And then the justice,
In fair round belly with good capon lined,
With eyes severe and beard of formal cut,
Full of wise saws and modern instances,
And so he plays his part. The sixth age shifts
Into the lean and slippered pantaloon,
With spectacles on nose and pouch on side,
His youthful hose well saved, a world too wide
For his shrunk shank, and his big manly voice
Turning again toward childish treble, pipes
And whistles in his sound. Last scene of all
That ends this strange, eventful history
Is second childishness and mere oblivion,
Sans teeth, sans eyes, sans taste, sans everything.
          (Act 2, Scene 7)

AMIENS
Blow, blow, thou winter wind,
Thou art not so unkind
    As man's ingratitude.
Thy tooth is not so keen
because thou art not seen,
    Although thy breath be rude.

Hey ho, sing hey ho, unto the green holly,
Most friendship is feigning, most loving mere folly.
    Then hey ho the holly,
    This life is most jolly.

Freeze, freeze, thou bitter sky
That dost not bite so nigh
    As benefits forgot.
Though thou the waters warp,
Thy sting is not so sharp
    As friend remembered not.

Hey ho, sing hey ho, unto the green holly,
Most friendship is feigning, most loving mere folly.
    Then hey ho the holly,
    This life is most jolly.

(Act 2, Scene 7)

CORIOLANUS

This double worship,
Where one part does disdain with cause, the other
Insult without all reason, where gentry, title, wisdom
Cannot conclude but by the yea and no
Of general ignorance, it must omit
Real necessities, and give way the while
To unstable slightness. Purpose so barred, it follows
Nothing is done to purpose. Therefore beseech you—
You that will be less fearful than discreet,
That love the fundamental part of state
More than you doubt the change on't, that prefer
A noble life before a long, and wish
To jump a body with a dangerous physic
That's sure of death without it—at once pluck out
The multitudinous tongue, let them not lick
The sweet which is their poison. Your dishonour
Mangles true judgment, and bereaves the state
Of that integrity which should become't,
Not having the power to do the good it would
For th'ill which doth control't.

(Act 3, Scene 1)

12

CORIOLANUS
You common cry of curs, whose breath I hate
As reek o'th' rotten fens, whose loves I prize
As the dead carcasses of unburied men
That do corrupt my air: I banish you.
And here remain with your uncertainty.
Let every feeble rumour shake your hearts.
Your enemies, with nodding of their plumes,
Fan you into despair. Have the power still
To banish your defenders, till at length
Your ignorance, which finds not till it feels,
Making but reservation of yourselves,
Still your own foes, deliver you
As most abated captives to some nation
That won you without blows. Despising
For you the city, thus I turn my back.
There is a world elsewhere.

(Act 3, Scene 3)

GIACOMO

What, are men mad? Hath nature given them eyes
To see this vaulted arch and the rich crop
Of sea and land, which can distinguish 'twixt
The fiery orbs above and the twinned stones
Upon th'unnumbered beach, and can we not
Partition make with spectacles so precious
'Twixt fair and foul?...
It cannot be i'th' eye, for apes and monkeys
'Twixt two such shes would chatter this way and
Contemn with mows the other. Nor i'th' judgment,
For idiots in this case of favour would
Be wisely definite. Nor i'th' appetite—
Sluttery, to such neat excellence opposed,
Should make desire vomit emptiness,
Not so allured to feed...
                              The cloyèd will,
That satiate yet unsatisfied desire, that tub
Both filled and running, ravening first the lamb,
Longs after for the garbage.

(Act 1, Scene 6)

ARVIRAGUS

With fairest flowers,
Whilst summer lasts and I live here, Fidele,
I'll sweeten thy sad grave. Thou shalt not lack
The flower that's like thy face, pale primrose, nor
The azured harebell, like thy veins. No, nor
The leaf of eglantine, whom not to slander,
Outsweetened not thy breath. The ruddock would
With charitable bill—O bill sore shaming
Those rich-left heirs that let their fathers lie
Without a monument!—bring thee all this,
Yea, and furred moss besides, when flowers are none,
To winter-gown thy corpse.

(Scene 4, Act 2)

GUIDERIUS AND ARVIRAGUS
Fear no more the heat o'th' sun,
   Nor the furious winter's rages.
Thou thy worldly task hast done,
   Home art gone and ta'en thy wages.
Golden lads and girls all must,
As chimney-sweepers, come to dust.

Fear no more the frown o'th' great,
   Thou art past the tyrant's stroke.
Care no more to clothe and eat,
   To thee the reed is as the oak.
The sceptre, learning, physic, must
All follow this and come to dust.

Fear no more the lightning flash,
   Nor th'all-dreaded thunder-stone.
Fear not slander, censure rash.
   Thou hast finished joy and moan.
All lovers young, all lovers must
Consign to thee and come to dust.

No exorcizer harm thee,
Nor no witchcraft charm thee.
Ghost unlaid forbear thee.
Nothing ill come near thee.
Quiet consummation have,
And renownèd be thy grave.
          (Scene 4, Act 2)

HAMLET

O, that this too too solid flesh would melt,
Thaw, and resolve itself into a dew,
Or that the Everlasting had not fixed
His canon 'gainst self-slaughter. O God, O God!
How weary, stale, flat, and unprofitable
Seem to me all the uses of this world!
Fie on't, ah fie, fie! 'Tis an unweeded garden
That grows to seed; things rank and gross in nature
Possess it merely. That it should come to this,
But two months dead—nay, not so much, not two.
So excellent a King, that was to this
Hyperion to a satyr, so loving to my mother
That he might not beteem the winds of heaven
Visit her face too roughly. Heaven and earth,
Must I remember? Why, she would hang on him
As if increase of appetite had grown
By what it fed on, and yet within a month—
Let me not think on't. Frailty, thy name is woman.
A little month, or ere those shoes were old
With which she followed my poor father's body,
Like Niobe, all tears, why, she, even she—
O God! A beast that wants discourse of reason
Would have mourned longer. Married with mine uncle,
My father's brother, but no more like my father
Than I to Hercules. Within a month?
Ere yet the salt of most unrighteous tears
Had left the flushing of her gallèd eyes,
She married. O, most wicked speed, to post
With such dexterity to incestuous sheets.

It is not, nor it cannot, come to good.
But break, my heart, for I must hold my tongue.

(Act 1, Scene 2)

POLONIUS
                    There, my blessing with thee,
And these few precepts in thy memory
See thou character: Give thy thoughts no tongue,
Nor any unproportioned thought his act;
Be thou familiar, but by no means vulgar;
The friends thou hast and their adoption tried,
Grapple them to thy soul with hoops of steel,
But do not dull thy palm with entertainment
Of each new-hatched, unfledged comrade; beware
Of entrance to a quarrel, but being in
Bear't that th'opposèd may beware of thee;
Give every man thine ear, but few thy voice;
Take each man's censure, but reserve thy judgment;
Costly thy habit as thy purse can buy,
But not expressed in fancy—rich, not gaudy—
For the apparel oft proclaims the man,
And they in France of the best rank and station
Are of a most select and generous chief in that;
Neither a borrower nor a lender be,
For loan oft loses both itself and friend,
And borrowing dulls the edge of husbandry;
This above all: to thine own self be true,
And it must follow, as the night the day,
Thou canst not then be false to any man.
Farewell, my blessing season this in thee.
                              (Act 1, Scene 3)

HAMLET

I have of late, but wherefore I know not, lost all my
mirth, forgone all custom of exercise, and indeed it
goes so heavily with my disposition that this goodly
frame, the earth, seems to me a sterile promontory.
This most excellent canopy the air, look you, this
brave o'er-hanging firmament, this majestical roof
fretted with golden fire—why, it appears no other
thing to me than a foul and pestilent congregation
of vapours. What a piece of work is a man! How
noble in reason, how infinite in faculty, in form and
moving how express and admirable, in action how
like an angel, in apprehension how like a god. The
beauty of the world! The paragon of animals! And
yet, to me, what is this quintessence of dust?

(Act 2, Scene 2)

HAMLET

O, what a rogue and peasant slave am I!
Is it not monstrous that this player here,
But in a fiction, in a dream of passion,
Could force his soul so to his whole conceit
That from her working all his visage wanned,
Tears in his eyes, distraction in's aspect,
A broken voice, and his whole function suiting
With forms to his conceit? And all for nothing.
For Hecuba!
What's Hecuba to him, or he to Hecuba,
That he should weep for her? What would he do
Had he the motive and the cue for passion
That I have? He would drown the stage with tears
And cleave the general ear with horrid speech,
Make mad the guilty and appal the free,
Confound the ignorant and amaze indeed
The very faculty of eyes and ears. Yet I,
A dull and muddy-mettled rascal, peak
Like John-a-dreams, unpregnant of my cause,
And can say nothing—no, not for a King
Upon whose property and most dear life
A damned defeat was made. Am I a coward?
Who calls me villain, breaks my pate across,
Plucks off my beard and blows it in my face,
Tweaks me by th'nose, gives me the lie i'th' throat
As deep as to the lungs? Who does me this?
Ha? 'Swounds, I should take it. For it cannot be
But I am pigeon-livered and lack gall
To make oppression bitter, or ere this

I should 'a' fatted all the region kites
With this slave's offal. Bloody, bawdy villain!
Remorseless, treacherous, lecherous, kindless villain!
O, vengeance!
Why, what an ass am I? Ay, sure, this is most brave
That I, the son of the dear murderèd,
Prompted to my revenge by heaven and hell,
Must like a whore unpack my heart with words
And fall a-cursing like a very drab,
A scullion! Fie upon't! Foh!—About, my brain.
I have heard that guilty creatures sitting at a play
Have by the very cunning of the scene
Been struck so to the soul that presently
They have proclaimed their malefactions.
For murder, though it have no tongue, will speak
With most miraculous organ. I'll have these players
Play something like the murder of my father
Before mine uncle. I'll observe his looks,
I'll tent him to the quick. If a but blench,
I know my course. The spirit that I have seen
May be the devil, and the devil hath power
T'assume a pleasing shape; yea, and perhaps
Out of my weakness and my melancholy,
As he is very potent with such spirits,
Abuses me to damn me. I'll have grounds
More relative than this. The play's the thing
Wherein I'll catch the conscience of the King.

(Act 2, Scene 2)

HAMLET

To be, or not to be, that is the question:
Whether 'tis nobler in the mind to suffer
The slings and arrows of outrageous fortune,
Or to take arms against a sea of troubles
And, by opposing, end them. To die, to sleep,
No more. And by a sleep to say we end
The heartache and the thousand natural shocks
That flesh is heir to. 'Tis a consummation
Devoutly to be wished. To die, to sleep.
To sleep, perchance to dream—ay, there's the rub.
For in that sleep of death what dreams may come
When we have shuffled off this mortal coil
Must give us pause. There's the respect
That makes calamity of so long life.
For who would bear the whips and scorns of time,
Th'oppressor's wrong, the proud man's contumely,
The pangs of disprized love, the law's delay,
The insolence of office, and the spurns
That patient merit of th'unworthy takes,
When he himself might his quietus make
With a bare bodkin? Who would these fardels bear,
To grunt and sweat under a weary life,
But that the dread of something after death,
The undiscovered country from whose bourn
No traveller returns, puzzles the will,
And makes us rather bear those ills we have
Than fly to others that we know not of.
Thus conscience does make cowards of us all.
And thus the native hue of resolution

Is sicklied o'er with the pale cast of thought,
And enterprises of great pith and moment
With this regard their currents turn awry
And lose the name of action.

(Act 3, Scene 1)

HAMLET

Speak the speech, I pray you, as I pronounced it to you, trippingly on the tongue. But if you mouth it, as many of your players do, I had as lief the town-crier had spoke my lines. Nor do not saw the air too much with your hand thus, but use all gently. For in the very torrent, tempest, and, as I may say, the whirlwind of your passion, you must acquire and beget a temperance that may give it smoothness. O, it offends me to the soul to hear a robustious peri-wig-pated fellow tear a passion to tatters, to very rags, to split the ears of the groundlings, who, for the most part, are capable of nothing but inexplicable dumb shows and noise. I would have such a fellow whipped for o'erdoing Termagant. It out-Herods Herod. Pray you, avoid it.

Be not too tame, neither, but let your own discretion be your tutor. Suit the action to the word, the word to the action, with this special observance: that you o'erstep not the modesty of nature. For anything so overdone is from the purpose of playing, whose end, both at the first and now, was and is to hold as 'twere the mirror up to nature, to show virtue her own feature, scorn her own image, and the very age and body of the time his form and pressure. Now this overdone or come tardy off, though it make the unskilful laugh, cannot but make the judicious grieve, the censure of the which one must in your allowance o'erweigh a whole theatre of others. O, there be players that I have seen play, and heard others praise—and that highly, not to speak it profanely—that neither having the accent of Christians, nor the gate of Christian, pagan, nor no man, have so strutted and bellowed that I have thought some of nature's journeymen had made men, and not made them well, they imitated humanity so abominably.

And let those that play your clowns speak no more than is set down for them. For there be of them that will themselves laugh to set on some quantity of barren spectators to laugh too, though in the meantime some necessary question of the play be then to be considered. That's villainous, and shows a most pitiful ambition in the fool that uses it. Go, make you ready.

(Act 3, Scene 2)

KING CLAUDIUS

O, my offence is rank, it smells to heaven.
It hath the primal eldest curse upon't,
A brother's murder. Pray can I not,
Though inclination be as sharp as will;
My stronger guilt defeats my strong intent,
And like a man to double business bound
I stand in pause where I shall first begin,
And both neglect. What if this cursèd hand
Were thicker than itself with brother's blood,
Is there not rain enough in the sweet heavens
To wash it white as snow? Whereto serves mercy
But to confront the visage of offence?
And what's in prayer but this twofold force
To be forestallèd ere we come to fall,
Or pardoned being down? Then I'll look up.
My fault is past. But O, what form of prayer
Can serve my turn? 'Forgive me my foul murder'?
That cannot be, since I am still possessed
Of those effects for which I did the murder—
My crown, mine own ambition, and my queen.
May one be pardoned and retain th'offence?
In the corrupted currents of this world
Offence's gilded hand may shove by justice,
And oft 'tis seen the wicked prize itself
Buys out the law. But 'tis not so above,
There is no shuffling. There the action lies
In his true nature, and we ourselves compelled
Even to the teeth and forehead of our faults
To give in evidence. What then? What rests?

Try what repentance can. What can it not?
Yet what can it, when one cannot repent?
O wretched state! O bosom, black as death!
O limèd soul that, struggling to be free,
Art more engaged. Help, angels! Make assay.
Bow, stubborn knees, and heart with strings of steel
Be soft as sinews of the new-born babe.
All may be well.

(Act 3, Scene 3)

HAMLET
How all occasions do inform against me
And spur my dull revenge. What is a man
If his chief good and market of his time
Be but to sleep and feed? A beast, no more.
Sure, he that made us with such large discourse,
Looking before and after, gave us not
That capability and god-like reason
To fust in us unused. Now whether it be
Bestial oblivion, or some craven scruple
Of thinking too precisely on th'event—
A thought which, quartered, hath but one part wisdom
And ever three parts coward—I do not know
Why yet I live to say this thing's to do,
Sith I have cause, and will, and strength, and means
To do't. Examples gross as earth exhort me.
Witness this army of such mass and charge
Led by a delicate and tender prince,
Whose spirit with divine ambition puffed
Makes mouths at the invisible event,
Exposing what is mortal and unsure
To all that fortune, death, and danger dare,
Even for an eggshell. Rightly to be great
Is not to stir without great argument,
But greatly to find quarrel in a straw
When honour's at the stake. How stand I, then,
That have a father killed, a mother stained,
Excitements of my reason and my blood,
And let all sleep while, to my shame, I see
The imminent death of twenty thousand men

That, for a fantasy and trick of fame,
Go to their graves like beds, fight for a plot
Whereon the numbers cannot try the cause,
Which is not tomb enough and continent
To hide the slain. O, from this time forth,
My thoughts be bloody or be nothing worth.

(Act 4, Scene 4)

QUEEN GERTRUDE

There is a willow grows aslant a brook
That shows his hoar leaves in the glassy stream.
Therewith fantastic garlands did she make
Of crow-flowers, nettles, daisies, and long purples
That liberal shepherds give a grosser name,
But our cold maids do dead men's fingers call them.
There on the pendant boughs her crownet weeds
Clamb'ring to hang, an envious sliver broke,
When down the weedy trophies and herself
Fell in the weeping brook. Her clothes spread wide,
And mermaid-like a while they bore her up,
Which time she chanted snatches of old tunes,
As one incapable of her own distress,
Or like a creature native and indued
Unto that element. But long it could not be
Till that her garments, heavy with their drink,
Pulled the poor wretch from her melodious lay
To muddy death.

(Act 4, Scene 7)

HAMLET

Alas, poor Yorick. I knew him, Horatio. A fellow of infinite jest, of most excellent fancy. He hath borne me on his back a thousand times. And now, how abhorred my imagination is—my gorge rises at it. Here hung those lips that I have kissed I know not how oft. Where be your gibes now, your gambols, your songs, your flashes of merriment that were wont to set the table on a roar? Not one now to mock your own grinning? Quite chop-fallen? Now get you to my lady's chamber and tell her, let her paint an inch thick, to this favour she must come. Make her laugh at that.

(Act 5, Scene 1)

HAMLET

There's a special providence in the fall of a sparrow. If it be now, 'tis not to come. If it be not to come, it will be now. If it be not now, yet it will come. The readiness is all. Since no man has aught of what he leaves, what is't to leave betimes?

(Act 5, Scene 2)

PRINCE HARRY

I know you all, and will a while uphold
The unyoked humour of your idleness.
Yet herein will I imitate the sun,
Who doth permit the base contagious clouds
To smother up his beauty from the world,
That when he please again to be himself,
Being wanted he may be more wondered at
By breaking through the foul and ugly mists
Of vapours that did seem to strangle him.
If all the year were playing holidays,
To sport would be as tedious as to work.
But when they seldom come, they wished-for come,
And nothing pleaseth but rare accidents.
So when this loose behaviour I throw off
And pay the debt I never promisèd,
By how much better than my word I am,
By so much shall I falsify men's hopes.
And, like bright metal on a sullen ground,
My reformation, glitt'ring o'er my fault,
Shall show more goodly and attract more eyes
Than that which hath no foil to set it off.
I'll so offend to make offence a skill,
Redeeming time when men think least I will.

(Act 1, Scene 2)

HOTSPUR
But I remember, when the fight was done,
When I was dry with rage and extreme toil,
Breathless and faint, leaning upon my sword,
Came there a certain lord, neat and trimly dressed,
Fresh as a bridegroom, and his chin, new-reaped,
Showed like a stubble-land at harvest-home.
He was perfumèd like a milliner,
And 'twixt his finger and his thumb he held
A pouncet-box, which ever and anon
He gave his nose and took't away again,
Who therewith angry, when it next came there
Took it in snuff, and still he smiled and talked.
And as the soldiers bore dead bodies by,
He called them untaught knaves, unmannerly
To bring a slovenly unhandsome corpse
Betwixt the wind and his nobility.
With many holiday and lady terms
He questioned me, amongst the rest demanded
My prisoners in your majesty's behalf.
I then, all smarting with my wounds being cold,
To be so pestered with a popinjay,
Out of my grief and my impatience
Answered neglectingly, I know not what—
He should, or should not—for he made me mad
To see him shine so brisk and smell so sweet,
And talk so like a waiting gentlewoman
Of guns, and drums, and wounds—God save the mark!
And telling me the sovereignest thing on earth
Was parmacety for an inward bruise,

And that it was great pity, so it was,
This villainous saltpetre should be digged
Out of the bowels of the harmless earth,
Which many a good tall fellow had destroyed
So cowardly, and but for these vile guns
He would himself have been a soldier.

(Act 1, Scene 3)

FALSTAFF

What need I be so forward with him that calls not on me? Well, 'tis no matter, honour pricks me on. Yea, but how if honour prick me off when I come on? How then? Can honour set to a leg? No. Or an arm? No. Or take away the grief of a wound? No. Honour hath no skill in surgery, then? No. What is honour? A word. What is in that word honour? What is that honour? Air. A trim reckoning! Who hath it? He that died o' Wednesday. Doth he feel it? No. Doth he hear it? No. 'Tis insensible then? Yea, to the dead. But will it not live with the living? No. Why? Detraction will not suffer it, therefore I'll none of it. Honour is a mere scutcheon. And so ends my catechism.

(Act 5, Scene 1)

FALSTAFF

Good faith, this same young sober-blooded boy doth
not love me, nor a man cannot make him laugh. But
that's no marvel, he drinks no wine. There's never
none of these demure boys come to any proof. For
thin drink doth so overcool their blood, and making
many fish meals, that they fall into a kind of male
green-sickness, and then when they marry they get
wenches. They are generally fools and cowards,
which some of us should be, too, but for inflamma-
tion. A good sherry-sack hath a two fold operation
in it: It ascends me into the brain, dries me there all
the foolish and dull and crudy vapours which envi-
ron it, makes it apprehensive, quick, forgetive, full
of nimble, fiery, and delectable shapes, which, de-
livered o'er to the voice, the tongue—which is the
birth—becomes excellent wit. The second property of your excellent sherry is the warming of the
blood, which before, cold and settled, left the liver
white and pale—which is the badge of pusillanimity
and cowardice—but the sherry warms it, and makes
it course from the inwards to the parts' extremes.
It illuminateth the face, which, as a beacon, gives
warning to all the rest of this little kingdom, man,
to arm. And then the vital commoners and inland
petty spirits muster me all to their captain, the heart,
who, great and puffed up with his retinue, doth any
deed of courage. And this valour comes of sherry,
so that skill in the weapon is nothing without sack,
for that sets it a-work, and learning a mere hoard of

gold kept by a devil, till sack commences it and sets it in act and use. Hereof comes it that Prince Harry is valiant. For the cold blood he did naturally inherit of his father he hath, like lean, sterile, and bare land, manured, husbanded, and tilled with excellent endeavour of drinking good, and good store of fertile sherry, that he is become very hot and valiant. If I had a thousand sons, the first humane principle I would teach them should be to forswear thin potations, and to addict themselves to sack.

(Act 4, Scene 2)

KING HENRY
I stay too long by thee, I weary thee.
Dost thou so hunger for mine empty chair
That thou wilt needs invest thee with my honours
Before thy hour be ripe? O foolish youth,
Thou seek'st the greatness that will overwhelm thee.
Stay but a little, for my cloud of dignity
Is held from falling with so weak a wind
That it will quickly drop. My day is dim.
Thou hast stol'n that which after some few hours
Were thine, without offence, and at my death
Thou hast sealed up my expectation.
Thy life did manifest thou lovedst me not,
And thou wilt have me die assured of it.
Thou hidst a thousand daggers in thy thoughts
Whom thou hast whetted on thy stony heart
To stab at half an hour of my life.
What, canst thou not forbear me half an hour?
Then get thee gone and dig my grave thyself,
And bid the merry bells ring to thine ear
That thou art crownèd, not that I am dead.
Let all the tears that should bedew my hearse
Be drops of balm to sanctify thy head,
Only compound me with forgotten dust.
Give that which gave thee life unto the worms.
Pluck down my officers, break my decrees,
For now a time is come to mock at form.
Harry the Fifth is crowned. Up, vanity!
Down, royal state! All you sage counsellors, hence!
And to the English court assemble now

From every region, apes of idleness!
Now, neighbour confines, purge you of your scum.
Have you a ruffian that will swear, drink, dance,
Revel the night, rob, murder, and commit
The oldest sins the newest kind of ways?
Be happy, he will trouble you no more.
England shall double gild his treble guilt,
England shall give him office, honour, might.
For the fifth Harry from curbed license plucks
The muzzle of restraint, and the wild dog
Shall flesh his tooth on every innocent.
O my poor kingdom, sick with civil blows!
When that my care could not withhold thy riots,
What wilt thou do when riot is thy care?
O, thou wilt be a wilderness again,
Peopled with wolves, thy old inhabitants.

(Act 4, Scene 3)

PRINCE HARRY

My father is gone wild into his grave,
For in his tomb lie my affections.
And with his spirits sadly I survive
To mock the expectation of the world,
To frustrate prophecies, and to raze out
Rotten opinion, who hath writ me down
After my seeming. The tide of blood in me
Hath proudly flowed in vanity till now.
Now doth it turn, and ebb back to the sea,
Where it shall mingle with the state of floods,
And flow henceforth in formal majesty.

(Act 5, Scene 2)

CHORUS

O, for a muse of fire, that would ascend
The brightest heaven of invention.
A kingdom for a stage, princes to act,
And monarchs to behold the swelling scene.
Then should the warlike Harry, like himself,
Assume the port of Mars, and at his heels,
Leashed in like hounds, should famine, sword, and fire
Crouch for employment. But pardon, gentles all,
The flat unraisèd spirits that hath dared
On this unworthy scaffold to bring forth
So great an object. Can this cockpit hold
The vasty fields of France? Or may we cram
Within this wooden O the very casques
That did affright the air at Agincourt?
O pardon, since a crookèd figure may
Attest in little place a million,
And let us, ciphers to this great account,
On your imaginary forces work.
Suppose within the girdle of these walls
Are now confined two mighty monarchies,
Whose high uprearèd and abutting fronts
The perilous narrow ocean parts asunder.
Piece out our imperfections with your thoughts,
Into a thousand parts divide one man,
And make imaginary puissance.
Think, when we talk of horses, that you see them
Printing their proud hooves i'th' receiving earth.
For 'tis your thoughts that now must deck our kings,
Carry them here and there, jumping o'er times,

Turning th'accomplishment of many years
Into an hourglass—for the which supply,
Admit me Chorus to this history,
Who prologue-like your humble patience pray
Gently to hear, kindly to judge our play.

(Prologue)

HOSTESS

Nay, sure, he's not in hell, he's in Arthur's bosom,
if ever man went to Arthur's bosom. A made a finer
end, and went away an it had been any christom
child. A parted e'en just between twelve and one,
e'en at the turning o'th' tide. For after I saw him fum-
ble with the sheets, and play with flowers, and smile
upon his fingers end, I knew there was but one way.
For his nose was as sharp as a pen and a babbled of
green fields. 'How now, Sir John?' quoth I, 'What,
man? Be o' good cheer.' So a cried out, 'God, God,
God!' three or four times. Now I, to comfort him,
bid him a should not think of God, I hoped there was
no need to trouble himself with any such thoughts
yet. So a bad me lay more clothes on his feet. I put
my hand into the bed and felt them, and they were
as cold as any stone. Then I felt to his knees, and so
up'ard, and up'ard, and all was as cold as any stone.

(Act 2, Scene 3)

KING HENRY

Once more unto the breach, dear friends, once more,
Or close the wall up with our English dead.
In peace, there's nothing so becomes a man
As modest stillness and humility.
But when the blast of war blows in our ears,
Then imitate the action of the tiger:
Stiffen the sinews, conjure up the blood,
Disguise fair nature with hard-favoured rage.
Then lend the eye a terrible aspect,
Let it pry through the portage of the head
Like the brass canon. Let the brow o'erwhelm it
As fearfully as doth a gallèd rock
O'erhang and jutty his confounded base,
Swilled with the wild and wasteful ocean.
Now set the teeth and stretch the nostril wide,
Hold hard the breath and bend up every spirit
To his full height. On, on, you noblest English,
Whose blood is fet from fathers of war-proof,
Fathers that, like so many Alexanders,
Have in these parts from morn till even fought
And sheathed their swords for lack of argument.
Dishonour not your mothers. Now attest
That those whom you called fathers did beget you.
Be copy now to men of grosser blood
And teach them how to war. And you, good yeomen,
Whose limbs were made in England, show us here
The mettle of your pasture. Let us swear
That you are worth your breeding, which I doubt not,
For there is none of you so mean and base

That hath not noble lustre in your eyes.
I see you stand like greyhounds in the slips,
Straining upon the start. The game's afoot.
Follow your spirit, and upon this charge
Cry, 'God for Harry, England, and Saint George!'
(Act 3, Scene 1)

KING HENRY

                    For as I am a soldier,
A name that in my thoughts becomes me best,
If I begin the batt'ry once again
I will not leave the half-achieved Harfleur
Till in her ashes she lie burièd.
The gates of mercy shall be all shut up,
And the fleshed soldier, rough and hard of heart,
In liberty of bloody hand, shall range
With conscience wide as hell, mowing like grass
Your fresh fair virgins and your flow'ring infants.
What is it then to me if impious war,
Arrayed in flames like to the prince of fiends,
Do with his smirched complexion all fell feats
Enlinked to waste and desolation?
What is't to me when you yourselves are cause
If your pure maidens fall into the hand
Of hot and forcing violation?
What rein can hold licentious wickedness
When down the hill he holds his fierce carrier?
We may as bootless spend our vain command
Upon th'enragèd soldiers in their spoil
As send precepts to the leviathan
To come ashore. Therefore, you men of Harfleur,
Take pity of your town and of your people
Whiles yet my soldiers are in my command,
Whiles yet the cool and temperate wind of grace
O'erblows the filthy and contagious clouds
Of heady murder, spoil, and villainy.
If not, why in a moment look to see

The blind and bloody soldier with foul hand
Defile the locks of your shrill-shrieking daughters,
Your fathers taken by the silver beards
And their most reverend heads dashed to the walls,
Your naked infants spitted upon pikes
Whiles the mad mothers with their howls confused
Do break the clouds as did the wives of Jewry
At Herod's bloody-hunting slaughtermen.
What say you? Will you yield and this avoid?
Or, guilty in defence, be thus destroyed?

(Act 3, Scene 3)

CHORUS
Now entertain conjecture of a time
When creeping murmur and the poring dark
Fills the wide vessel of the universe.
From camp to camp, through the foul womb of night,
The hum of either army stilly sounds,
That the fixed sentinels almost receive
The secret whispers of each other's watch.
Fire answers fire, and through their paly flames
Each battle sees the other's umbered face.
Steed threatens steed in high and boastful neighs,
Piercing the night's dull ear. And from the tents,
The armourers accomplishing the knights,
With busy hammers closing rivets up,
Give dreadful note of preparation.
The country cocks do crow, the clocks do toll
And the third hour of drowsy morning name.
Proud of their numbers and secure in soul,
The confident and over-lusty French
Do the low-rated English play at dice
And chide the cripple tardy-gated night,
Who, like a foul and ugly witch, doth limp
So tediously away. The poor condemnèd English,
Like sacrifices, by their watchful fires
Sit patiently and inly ruminate
The morning's danger. And their gesture sad,
Investing lank-lean cheeks and war-worn coats,
Presented them unto the gazing moon
So many horrid ghosts. O, now who will behold
The royal captain of this ruined band

Walking from watch to watch, from tent to tent,
Let him cry, 'Praise and glory on his head!'
For forth he goes and visits all his host,
Bids them good morrow with a modest smile,
And calls them brothers, friends, and countrymen.
Upon his royal face there is no note
How dread an army hath enrounded him,
Nor doth he dedicate one jot of colour
Unto the weary and all-watchèd night,
But freshly looks and overbears attaint
With cheerful semblance and sweet majesty,
That every wretch, pining and pale before,
Beholding him plucks comfort from his looks.
A largess universal, like the sun,
His liberal eye doth give to every one,
Thawing cold fear, that mean and gentle all
Behold, as may unworthiness define,
A little touch of Harry in the night.

(Act 4, Prologue)

KING HENRY

Upon the King. 'Let us our lives, our souls,
Our debts, our careful wives,
Our children, and our sins, lay on the King.'
We must bear all. O hard condition,
Twin-born with greatness, subject to the breath
Of every fool whose sense no more can feel
But his own wringing. What infinite heart's-ease
Must kings neglect that private men enjoy?
And what have kings that privates have not too,
Save ceremony, save general ceremony?
And what art thou, thou idol ceremony?
What kind of god art thou that suffer'st more
Of mortal griefs than do thy worshippers?
What are thy rents? What are thy comings-in?
O ceremony, show me but thy worth.
What is thy soul of adoration?
Art thou ought else but place, degree, and form,
Creating awe and fear in other men?
Wherein thou art less happy, being feared,
Than they in fearing.
What drink'st thou oft, instead of homage sweet,
But poisoned flattery? O, be sick, great greatness,
And bid thy ceremony give thee cure.
Thinks thou the fiery fever will go out
With titles blown from adulation?
Will it give place to flexure and low bending?
Canst thou, when thou command'st the beggar's knee,
Command the health of it? No, thou proud dream
That play'st so subtly with a king's repose.

Henry V

I am a king that find thee, and I know
'Tis not the balm, the sceptre, and the ball,
The sword, the mace, the crown imperial,
The intertissued robe of gold and pearl,
The farcèd title running 'fore the king,
The throne he sits on, nor the tide of pomp
That beats upon the high shore of this world—
No, not all these, thrice-gorgeous ceremony,
Not all these laid in bed majestical
Can sleep so soundly as the wretched slave,
Who with a body filled and vacant mind
Gets him to rest crammed with distressful bread;
Never sees horrid night, the child of hell,
But like a lackey from the rise to set
Sweats in the eye of Phoebus and all night
Sleeps in Elysium; next day after dawn
Doth rise and help Hyperion to his horse,
And follows so the ever-running year
With profitable labour to his grave.
And but for ceremony, such a wretch,
Winding up days with toil and nights with sleep,
Had the forehand and vantage of a king.
The slave, a member of the country's peace,
Enjoys it, but in gross brain little wots
What watch the King keeps to maintain the peace,
Whose hours the peasant best advantages.

(Act 4, Scene 1)

KING HENRY

If we are marked to die, we are enough
To do our country loss. And if to live,
The fewer men the greater share of honour.
God's will, I pray thee wish not one man more.
By Jove, I am not covetous for gold,
Nor care I who doth feed upon my cost.
It earns me not if men my garments wear.
Such outward things dwell not in my desires.
But if it be a sin to covet honour,
I am the most offending soul alive.
No, faith, my coz, wish not a man from England.
God's peace, I would not lose so great an honour
As one man more methinks would share from me,
For the best hope I have. O, do not wish one more,
Rather proclaim it presently through my host
That he which hath no stomach to this fight,
Let him depart. His passport shall be made,
And crowns for convoy put into his purse.
We would not die in that man's company
That fears his fellowship to die with us.
This day is called the Feast of Crispian.
He that outlives this day and comes safe home
Will stand a tip-toe when this day is named
And rouse him at the name of Crispian.
He that shall see this day and live t'old age
Will yearly on the vigil feast his neighbours
And say, 'Tomorrow is Saint Crispian.'
Then will he strip his sleeve and show his scars
And say, 'These wounds I had on Crispin's day.'

Old men forget, yet all shall be forgot
But he'll remember with advantages
What feats he did that day. Then shall our names,
Familiar in his mouth as household words—
Harry the King, Bedford and Exeter,
Warwick and Talbot, Salisbury and Gloucester—
Be in their flowing cups freshly remembered.
This story shall the good man teach his son.
And Crispin Crispian shall ne'er go by
From this day to the ending of the world,
But we in it shall be rememberèd,
We few, we happy few, we band of brothers—
For he today that sheds his blood with me
Shall be my brother, be he ne'er so vile
This day shall gentle his condition.
And gentlemen in England now abed
Shall think themselves accursed they were not here,
And hold their manhoods cheap whiles any speaks
That fought with us upon Saint Crispin's day.

(Act 4, Scene 3)

KING HENRY
This battle fares like to the morning's war,
When dying clouds contend with growing light,
What time the shepherd, blowing of his nails,
Can neither call it perfect day nor night.
Now sways it this way, like a mighty sea
Forced by the tide to combat with the wind.
Now sways it that way, like the selfsame sea
Forced to retire by fury of the wind.
Sometime the flood prevails, and then the wind.
Now one the better, then another best,
Both tugging to be victors, breast to breast,
Yet neither conqueror nor conquerèd.
So is the equal poise of this fell war.
Here on this molehill will I sit me down.
To whom God will, there be the victory.
For Margaret my queen, and Clifford, too,
Have chid me from the battle, swearing both
They prosper best of all when I am thence.
Would I were dead, if God's good will were so,
For what is in this world but grief and woe?
O God! Methinks it were a happy life
To be no better than a homely swain,
To sit upon a hill, as I do now,
To carve out dials quaintly, point by point,
Thereby to see the minutes how they run:
How many makes the hour full complete,
How many hours brings about the day,
How many days will finish up the year,
How many years a mortal man may live.

When this is known, then to divide the times:
So many hours must I tend my flock,
So many hours must I take my rest,
So many hours must I contemplate,
So many hours must I sport myself,
So many days my ewes have been with young,
So many weeks ere the poor fools will ean,
So many years ere I shall shear the fleece.
So minutes, hours, days, weeks, months, and years,
Passed over to the end they were created,
Would bring white hairs unto a quiet grave.
Ah, what a life were this! How sweet! How lovely!
Gives not the hawthorn bush a sweeter shade
To shepherds looking on their silly sheep
Than doth a rich embroidered canopy
To kings that fear their subjects' treachery?
O yes, it doth, a thousand fold it doth.
And to conclude, the shepherd's homely curds,
His cold thin drink out of his leather bottle,
His wonted sleep under a fresh tree's shade,
All, which secure and sweetly he enjoys,
Is far beyond a prince's delicates,
His viands sparkling in a golden cup,
His body couchèd in a curious bed,
When care, mistrust, and treason waits on him.

(Act 2, Scene 5)

RICHARD OF GLOUCESTER
Well, say there is no kingdom then for Richard,
What other pleasure can the world afford?
I'll make my heaven in a lady's lap,
And deck my body in gay ornaments,
And 'witch sweet ladies with my words and looks.
O, miserable thought! And more unlikely
Than to accomplish twenty golden crowns.
Why, love forswore me in my mother's womb,
And, for I should not deal in her soft laws,
She did corrupt frail nature with some bribe
To shrink mine arm up like a withered shrub,
To make an envious mountain on my back
Where sits deformity to mock my body,
To shape my legs of an unequal size,
To disproportion me in every part
Like to a chaos, or an unlicked bear whelp
That carries no impression like the dam.
And am I then a man to be beloved?
O, monstrous fault, to harbour such a thought!
Then, since this earth affords no joy to me
But to command, to check, to o'erbear such
As are of better person than myself,
I'll make my heaven to dream upon the crown,
And whiles I live, t'account this world but hell,
Until my misshaped trunk that bears this head
Be round impalèd with a glorious crown.
And yet I know not how to get the crown,
For many lives stand between me and home.
And I, like one lost in a thorny wood,

That rents the thorns and is rent with the thorns,
Seeking a way and straying from the way,
Not knowing how to find the open air
But toiling desperately to find it out,
Torment myself to catch the English crown.
And from that torment I will free myself,
Or hew my way out with a bloody axe.
Why, I can smile, and murder whiles I smile,
And cry 'Content!' to that which grieves my heart,
And wet my cheeks with artificial tears,
And frame my face to all occasions.
I'll drown more sailors than the mermaid shall,
I'll slay more gazers than the basilisk,
I'll play the orator as well as Nestor,
Deceive more slyly than Ulysses could,
And, like a Sinon, take another Troy.
I can add colours to the chameleon,
Change shapes with Proteus for advantages,
And set the murderous Machiavel to school.
Can I do this, and cannot get a crown?
Tut, were it farther off, I'll pluck it down.

(Act 3, Scene 2)

CASSIUS
I cannot tell what you and other men
Think of this life. But for my single self,
I had as lief not be, as live to be
In awe of such a thing as I myself.
I was born free as Caesar—so were you.
We both have fed as well, and we can both
Endure the winter's cold as well as he.
For once, upon a raw and gusty day,
The troubled Tiber chafing with her shores,
Caesar said to me, 'Dar'st thou, Cassius, now
Leap in with me into this angry flood
And swim to yonder point?' Upon the word,
Accoutred as I was, I plungèd in
And bade him follow. So indeed he did.
The torrent roared and we did buffet it
With lusty sinews, throwing it aside,
And stemming it with hearts of controversy.
But ere we could arrive the point proposed,
Caesar cried, 'Help me, Cassius, or I sink!'
Ay, as Aeneas our great ancestor
Did from the flames of Troy upon his shoulder
The old Anchises bear, so from the waves of Tiber
Did I the tirèd Caesar. And this man
Is now become a god, and Cassius is
A wretched creature and must bend his body
If Caesar carelessly but nod on him.
He had a fever when he was in Spain,
And when the fit was on him I did mark
How he did shake. 'Tis true, this god did shake.

His coward lips did from their colour fly,
And that same eye, whose bend doth awe the world,
Did lose his lustre. I did hear him groan,
Ay, and that tongue of his that bade the Romans
Mark him and write his speeches in their books,
'Alas!' it cried, 'Give me some drink, Titinius!'
As a sick girl. Ye gods, it doth amaze me
A man of such a feeble temper should
So get the start of the majestic world
And bear the palm alone.

(Act 1, Scene 2)

BRUTUS
It must be by his death. And for my part,
I know no personal cause to spurn at him,
But for the general. He would be crowned—
How that might change his nature, there's the question.
It is the bright day that brings forth the adder
And that craves wary walking. Crown him, that!
And then I grant we put a sting in him
That at his will he may do danger with.
Th'abuse of greatness is when it disjoins
Remorse from power. And to speak truth of Caesar,
I have not known when his affections swayed
More than his reason. But 'tis a common proof
That lowliness is young ambition's ladder
Whereto the climber upward turns his face;
But when he once attains the upmost round
He then unto the ladder turns his back,
Looks in the clouds, scorning the base degrees
By which he did ascend. So Caesar may.
Then lest he may, prevent. And since the quarrel
Will bear no colour for the thing he is,
Fashion it thus: that what he is, augmented,
Would run to these and these extremities.
And therefore think him as a serpent's egg,
Which, hatched, would as his kind grow mischievous,
And kill him in the shell.

(*Act 2, Scene 1*)

BRUTUS
No, not an oath. If not the face of men,
The sufferance of our souls, the time's abuse —
If these be motives weak, break off betimes
And every man hence to his idle bed.
So let high-sighted tyranny range on
Till each man drop by lottery. But if these,
As I am sure they do, bear fire enough
To kindle cowards and to steel with valour
The melting spirits of women, then, countrymen,
What need we any spur but our own cause
To prick us to redress? What other bond
Than secret Romans that have spoke the word
And will not palter? And what other oath
Than honesty to honesty engaged
That this shall be, or we will fall for it?
Swear priests and cowards and men cautelous,
Old feeble carrions and such suffering souls
That welcome wrongs; unto bad causes swear
Such creatures as men doubt. But do not stain
The even virtue of our enterprise,
Nor th'insuppressive mettle of our spirits,
To think that or our cause or our performance
Did need an oath, when every drop of blood
That every Roman bears, and nobly bears,
Is guilty of a several bastardy
If he do break the smallest particle
Of any promise that hath past from him.

(*Act 2, Scene 1*)

BRUTUS
Our course will seem too bloody, Caius Cassius,
To cut the head off and then hack the limbs,
Like wrath in death and envy afterwards,
For Antony is but a limb of Caesar.
Let's be sacrificers, but not butchers, Caius.
We all stand up against the spirit of Caesar,
And in the spirit of men there is no blood.
O, that we then could come by Caesar's spirit
And not dismember Caesar! But, alas,
Caesar must bleed for it. And, gentle friends,
Let's kill him boldly, but not wrathfully.
Let's carve him as a dish fit for the gods,
Not hew him as a carcass fit for hounds.
And let our hearts, as subtle masters do,
Stir up their servants to an act of rage,
And after seem to chide 'em. This shall make
Our purpose necessary and not envious,
Which so appearing to the common eyes
We shall be called purgers, not murderers.
And for Marc Antony, think not of him,
For he can do no more than Caesar's arm
When Caesar's head is off.

(Act 2, Scene 1)

CAESAR

Cowards die many times before their deaths;
The valiant never taste of death but once.
Of all the wonders that I yet have heard,
It seems to me most strange that men should fear,
Seeing that death, a necessary end,
Will come when it will come.

(Act 2, Scene 2)

ANTONY

O, pardon me, thou bleeding piece of earth,
That I am meek and gentle with these butchers.
Thou art the ruins of the noblest man
That ever livèd in the tide of times.
Woe to the hand that shed this costly blood!
Over thy wounds now do I prophesy,
Which like dumb mouths do ope' their ruby lips
To beg the voice and utterance of my tongue:
A curse shall light upon the limbs of men;
Domestic fury and fierce civil strife
Shall cumber all the parts of Italy;
Blood and destruction shall be so in use,
And dreadful objects so familiar,
That mothers shall but smile when they behold
Their infants quartered with the hands of war,
All pity choked with custom of fell deeds;
And Caesar's spirit, ranging for revenge,
With Ate by his side come hot from hell,
Shall in these confines with a monarch's voice
Cry 'Havoc!' and let slip the dogs of war,
That this foul deed shall smell above the earth
With carrion men, groaning for burial.

(Act 3, Scene 1)

ANTONY

Friends, Romans, countrymen, lend me your ears.
I come to bury Caesar, not to praise him.
The evil that men do lives after them,
The good is oft interrèd with their bones.
So let it be with Caesar. The noble Brutus
Hath told you Caesar was ambitious.
If it were so, it was a grievous fault,
And grievously hath Caesar answered it.
Here, under leave of Brutus and the rest—
For Brutus is an honourable man,
So are they all, all honourable men—
Come I to speak in Caesar's funeral.
He was my friend, faithful and just to me.
But Brutus says he was ambitious,
And Brutus is an honourable man.
He hath brought many captives home to Rome
Whose ransoms did the general coffers fill.
Did this in Caesar seem ambitious?
When that the poor have cried, Caesar hath wept.
Ambition should be made of sterner stuff.
Yet Brutus says he was ambitious,
And Brutus is an honourable man.
You all did see that on the Lupercal
I thrice presented him a kingly crown
Which he did thrice refuse. Was this ambition?
Yet Brutus says he was ambitious,
And sure he is an honourable man.
I speak not to disprove what Brutus spoke,
But here I am to speak what I do know.

You all did love him once, not without cause.
What cause withholds you then to mourn for him?
O judgment! Thou art fled to brutish beasts
And men have lost their reason. Bear with me,
My heart is in the coffin there with Caesar,
And I must pause till it come back to me.

(Act 3, Scene 2)

CONSTANCE
Grief fills the room up of my absent child,
Lies in his bed, walks up and down with me,
Puts on his pretty looks, repeats his words,
Remembers me of all his gracious parts,
Stuffs out his vacant garments with his form.
Then have I reason to be fond of grief?
Fare you well. Had you such a loss as I,
I could give better comfort than you do.
I will not keep this form upon my head
When there is such disorder in my wit.
O Lord, my boy, my Arthur, my fair son,
My life, my joy, my food, my all the world,
My widow-comfort, and my sorrow's cure!
                                    (Act 3, Scene 4)

EDMOND

Thou, nature, art my goddess. To thy law
My services are bound. Wherefore should I
Stand in the plague of custom and permit
The curiosity of nations to deprive me?
For that I am some twelve or fourteen moonshines
Lag of a brother? Why bastard? Wherefore base?
When my dimensions are as well compact,
My mind as generous, and my shape as true
As honest madam's issue? Why brand they us
With base? With baseness, bastardy? Base, base?
Who in the lusty stealth of nature take
More composition and fierce quality
Than doth within a dull stale tirèd bed
Go to th'creating a whole tribe of fops
Got 'tween a sleep and wake? Well then,
Legitimate Edgar, I must have your land.
Our father's love is to the bastard Edmond
As to th'legitimate. Fine word, 'legitimate'.
Well, my legitimate, if this letter speed
And my invention thrive, Edmond the base
Shall to th'legitimate. I grow, I prosper.
Now gods, stand up for bastards!

(Act 1, Scene 2)

70

LEAR

Hear, nature, hear, dear goddess, hear:
Suspend thy purpose if thou did'st intend
To make this creature fruitful.
Into her womb convey sterility,
Dry up in her the organs of increase,
And from her derogate body never spring
A babe to honor her. If she must teem,
Create her child of spleen, that it may live
And be a thwart disnatured torment to her.
Let it stamp wrinkles in her brow of youth,
With cadent tears fret channels in her cheeks,
Turn all her mother's pains and benefits
To laughter and contempt, that she may feel
How sharper than a serpent's tooth it is
To have a thankless child. Away, away!

(Act 1, Scene 4)

LEAR

O, reason not the need! Our basest beggars
Are in the poorest thing superfluous.
Allow not nature more than nature needs,
Man's life is cheap as beast's. Thou art a lady.
If only to go warm were gorgeous,
Why, nature needs not what thou gorgeous wear'st,
Which scarcely keeps thee warm. But for true need—
You heavens, give me that patience, patience I need.
You see me here, you gods, a poor old man,
As full of grief as age, wretched in both.
If it be you that stirs these daughters' hearts
Against their father, fool me not so much
To bear it tamely. Touch me with noble anger,
And let not women's weapons, water drops,
Stain my man's cheeks. No, you unnatural hags,
I will have such revenges on you both
That all the world shall—I will do such things—
What they are yet I know not, but they shall be
The terrors of the earth. You think I'll weep?
No, I'll not weep. I have full cause of weeping,
But this heart shall break into a hundred thousand flaws
Or ere I'll weep. O fool, I shall go mad!

(Act 2, Scene 2)

LEAR

Blow, winds, and crack your cheeks! Rage, blow,
You cataracts and hurricanoes, spout
Till you have drenched our steeples, drowned the cocks!
You sulph'rous and thought-executing fires,
Vaunt-couriers of oak-cleaving thunderbolts,
Singe my white head! And thou all-shaking thunder,
Strike flat the thick rotundity o'th' world,
Crack nature's moulds, all germens spill at once
That makes ingrateful man!

(Act 3, Scene 2)

LEAR

Poor naked wretches, wheresoe'er you are,
That bide the pelting of this pitiless storm,
How shall your houseless heads and unfed sides,
Your looped and windowed raggedness, defend you
From seasons such as these? O, I have ta'en
Too little care of this. Take physic, pomp,
Expose thyself to feel what wretches feel,
That thou may'st shake the superflux to them
And show the heavens more just.

(Act 3, Scene 4)

LEAR

Thou wert better in a grave than to answer with thy uncovered body this extremity of the skies. Is man no more than this? Consider him well. Thou owest the worm no silk, the beast no hide, the sheep no wool, the cat no perfume. Ha! Here's three on's are sophisticated, thou art the thing itself. Unaccommodated man is no more but such a poor, bare, forked animal as thou art. Off, off you lendings! Come, unbutton here.

(Act 3, Scene 4)

EDGAR

                            How fearful
And dizzy 'tis to cast one's eyes so low.
The crows and choughs that wing the midway air
Show scarce so gross as beetles. Halfway down
Hangs one that gathers samphire, dreadful trade.
Methinks he seems no bigger than his head.
The fishermen that walk upon the beach
Appear like mice, and yon tall anchoring barque
Diminished to her cock, her cock a buoy
Almost too small for sight. The murmuring surge
That on th'unnumbered idle pebble chafes
Cannot be heard so high. I'll look no more
Lest my brain turn and the deficient sight
Topple down headlong.

                                 (Act 4, Scene 5)

LEAR

No, no, no, no. Come, let's away to prison.
We two alone will sing like birds i'th' cage.
When thou dost ask me blessing, I'll kneel down
And ask of thee forgiveness. So we'll live,
And pray, and sing, and tell old tales, and laugh
At gilded butterflies, and hear poor rogues
Talk of court news, and we'll talk with them, too—
Who loses and who wins, who's in, who's out—
And take upon's the mystery of things
As if we were God's spies. And we'll wear out
In a walled prison packs and sects of great ones
That ebb and flow by th'moon.

(Act 5, Scene 3)

BEROWNE

Other slow arts entirely keep the brain,
And therefore, finding barren practisers,
Scarce show a harvest of their heavy toil.
But love, first learnèd in a lady's eyes,
Lives not alone immurèd in the brain,
But with the motion of all elements
Courses as swift as thought in every power,
And gives to every power a double power
Above their functions and their offices:
It adds a precious seeing to the eye;
A lover's eyes will gaze an eagle blind.
A lover's ear will hear the lowest sound
When the suspicious head of theft is stopped.
Love's feeling is more soft and sensible
Than are the tender horns of cockled snails.
Love's tongue proves dainty Bacchus gross in taste.
For valour, is not love a Hercules,
Still climbing trees in the Hesperides?
Subtle as Sphinx, as sweet and musical
As bright Apollo's lute strung with his hair.
And when love speaks, the voice of all the gods
Make heaven drowsy with the harmony.
Never durst poet touch a pen to write
Until his ink were tempered with love's sighs;
O, then his lines would ravish savage ears
And plant in tyrants mild humility.
From women's eyes this doctrine I derive:
They sparkle still the right Promethean fire.
They are the books, the arts, the academes,

That show, contain, and nourish all the world,
Else none at all in aught proves excellent.

(Act 4, Scene 3)

SPRING

When daisies pied and violets blue,
    And lady-smocks all silver white,
And cuckoo-buds of yellow hue,
    Do paint the meadows with delight,
The cuckoo then on every tree
Mocks married men, for thus sings he:
    Cuckoo!
Cuckoo, cuckoo! O word of fear,
Unpleasing to a married ear.

When shepherds pipe on oaten straws,
    And merry larks are ploughmen's clocks,
When turtles tread, and rooks and daws,
    And maidens bleach their summer smocks,
The cuckoo then on every tree
Mocks married men, for thus sings he:
    Cuckoo!
Cuckoo, cuckoo! O word of fear,
Unpleasing to a married ear.

(Act 5, Scene 2)

WINTER
When icicles hang by the wall,
    And Dick the shepherd blows his nail,
And Tom bears logs into the hall,
    And milk comes frozen home in pail,
When blood is nipped and ways be foul,
Then nightly sings the staring owl:
Tu-whit, tu-whoo! A merry note,
While greasy Joan doth keel the pot.

When all aloud the wind doth blow,
    And coughing drowns the parson's saw,
And birds sit brooding in the snow,
    And Marian's nose looks red and raw,
When roasted crabs hiss in the bowl,
Then nightly sings the staring owl:
Tu-whit, tu-whoo! A merry note,
While greasy Joan doth keel the pot.
                                    (Act 5, Scene 2)

MACBETH
This supernatural soliciting
Cannot be ill, cannot be good. If ill,
Why hath it given me earnest of success
Commencing in a truth? I am Thane of Cawdor.
If good, why do I yield to that suggestion
Whose horrid image doth unfix my hair,
And make my seated heart knock at my ribs
Against the use of nature? Present fears
Are less than horrible imaginings.
My thought, whose murder yet is but fantastical,
Shakes so my single state of man
That function is smothered in surmise,
And nothing is but what is not.

(Act 1, Scene 3)

LADY MACBETH
                    The raven himself is hoarse
That croaks the fatal entrance of Duncan
Under my battlements. Come, you spirits
That tend on mortal thoughts, unsex me here,
And fill me from the crown to the toe top-full
Of direst cruelty. Make thick my blood,
Stop up th'access and passage to remorse,
That no compunctious visitings of nature
Shake my fell purpose, nor keep peace between
Th'effect and it. Come to my woman's breasts
And take my milk for gall, you murd'ring ministers,
Wherever in your sightless substances
You wait on nature's mischief. Come, thick night,
And pall thee in the dunnest smoke of hell,
That my keen knife see not the wound it makes,
Nor heaven peep through the blanket of the dark
To cry, 'Hold, hold!'
                                    (Act 1, Scene 5)

MACBETH

If it were done when 'tis done, then 'twere well
It were done quickly. If th'assassination
Could trammel up the consequence, and catch
With his surcease success, that but this blow
Might be the be-all and the end-all, here,
But here upon this bank and shoal of time,
We'd jump the life to come. But in these cases
We still have judgment here, that we but teach
Bloody instructions which, being taught, return
To plague th'inventer. This even-handed justice
Commends th'ingredients of our poisoned chalice
To our own lips. He's here in double trust:
First, as I am his kinsman and his subject,
Strong both against the deed. Then, as his host
Who should against his murderer shut the door,
Not bear the knife myself. Besides, this Duncan
Hath borne his faculties so meek, hath been
So clear in his great office, that his virtues
Will plead like angels, trumpet-tongued against
The deep damnation of his taking off.
And pity, like a naked new-born babe
Striding the blast, or heaven's cherubin horsed
Upon the sightless curriers of the air,
Shall blow the horrid deed in every eye,
That tears shall drown the wind. I have no spur
To prick the sides of my intent, but only
Vaulting ambition, which o'er-leaps itself
And falls on th'other.

(Act 1, Scene 7)

LADY MACBETH

Was the hope drunk
Wherein you dressed yourself? Hath it slept since?
And wakes it now to look so green and pale
At what it did so freely? From this time
Such I account thy love. Art thou afeared
To be the same in thine own act and valour
As thou art in desire? Would'st thou have that
Which thou esteem'st the ornament of life,
And live a coward in thine own esteem,
Letting 'I dare not' wait upon 'I would',
Like the poor cat i'th' adage?...

What beast was't then
That made you break this enterprise to me?
When you durst do it, then you were a man.
And to be more than what you were, you would
Be so much more the man. Nor time nor place
Did then adhere, and yet you would make both.
They have made themselves, and that their fitness now
Does unmake you. I have given suck, and know
How tender 'tis to love the babe that milks me.
I would, while it was smiling in my face,
Have plucked my nipple from his boneless gums
And dashed the brains out, had I so sworn
As you have done to this.

(Act 1, Scene 7)

MACBETH
Is this a dagger which I see before me,
The handle toward my hand? Come, let me clutch thee.
I have thee not, and yet I see thee still.
Art thou not, fatal vision, sensible
To feeling as to sight? Or art thou but
A dagger of the mind, a false creation
Proceeding from the heat-oppressèd brain?
I see thee yet, in form as palpable
As this which now I draw.
Thou marshall'st me the way that I was going,
And such an instrument I was to use.
Mine eyes are made the fools o'th' other senses,
Or else worth all the rest. I see thee still,
And on thy blade and dudgeon gouts of blood,
Which was not so before. There's no such thing.
It is the bloody business which informs
Thus to mine eyes. Now o'er the one half world
Nature seems dead, and wicked dreams abuse
The curtained sleep. Witchcraft celebrates
Pale Hecate's offerings, and withered murder,
Alarumed by his sentinel the wolf,
Whose howl's his watch, thus with his stealthy pace,
With Tarquin's ravishing strides, towards his design
Moves like a ghost. Thou sure and firm-set earth,
Hear not my steps which way they walk, for fear
Thy very stones prate of my whereabout,
And take the present horror from the time,

Which now suits with it. Whiles I threat, he lives.
Words to the heat of deeds too cold breath gives.

(Act 2, Scene 1)

Macbeth

LENNOX

The night has been unruly. Where we lay
Our chimneys were blown down, and, as they say,
Lamentings heard i'th' air, strange screams of death,
And prophesying with accents terrible
Of dire combustion and confused events,
New hatched to th'woeful time. The obscure bird
Clamoured the livelong night. Some say the earth
Was feverous and did shake.

(Act 2, Scene 3)

MACBETH

Had I but died an hour before this chance,
I had lived a blessèd time. For from this instant,
There's nothing serious in mortality.
All is but toys. Renown and grace is dead.
The wine of life is drawn, and the mere lees
Is left this vault to brag of.

(Act 2, Scene 3)

WITCHES
Thrice the brinded cat hath mewed.
Thrice, and once the hedge-pig whined.
Harpier cries ''Tis time, 'tis time.'

Round about the cauldron go,
In the poisoned entrails throw.
Toad, that under cold stone
Days and nights has thirty-one
Sweltered venom sleeping got,
Boil thou first i'th' charmèd pot.
    Double, double, toil and trouble,
    Fire burn, and cauldron bubble.

Fillet of a fenny snake,
In the cauldron boil and bake.
Eye of newt and toe of frog,
Wool of bat and tongue of dog,
Adder's fork and blind-worm's sting,
Lizard's leg and owlet's wing.
For a charm of powerful trouble,
Like a hell-broth boil and bubble.
    Double, double, toil and trouble,
    Fire burn, and cauldron bubble.

Scale of dragon, tooth of wolf,
Witches' mummy, maw and gulf
Of the ravined salt-sea shark,
Root of hemlock digged i'th' dark,
Liver of blaspheming Jew,

Gall of goat, and slips of yew
Slivered in the moon's eclipse,
Nose of Turk and Tartar's lips,
Finger of birth-strangled babe
Ditch-delivered by a drab.
Make the gruel thick and slab.
Add thereto a tiger's chaudron,
For th'ingredients of our cauldron.
   Double, double, toil and trouble,
   Fire burn, and cauldron bubble.

Cool it with a baboon's blood,
Then the charm is firm and good.

(Act 4, Scene 1)

MACBETH
I have lived long enough. My way of life
Is fall'n into the sere, the yellow leaf.
And that which should accompany old age,
As honour, love, obedience, troops of friends,
I must not look to have, but in their stead
Curses, not loud but deep, mouth-honour, breath
Which the poor heart would fain deny, and dare not.

(Act 5, Scene 3)

MACBETH

Tomorrow, and tomorrow, and tomorrow
Creeps in this petty pace from day to day
To the last syllable of recorded time.
And all our yesterdays have lighted fools
The way to dusty death. Out, out, brief candle.
Life's but a walking shadow, a poor player
That struts and frets his hour upon the stage,
And then is heard no more. It is a tale
Told by an idiot, full of sound and fury,
Signifying nothing.

(Act 5, Scene 5)

ISABELLA

Could great men thunder
As Jove himself does, Jove would never be quiet,
For every pelting petty officer
Would use his heaven for thunder, nothing but thunder.
Merciful heaven,
Thou rather with thy sharp and sulphurous bolt
Split'st the unwedgeable and gnarlèd oak
Than the soft myrtle. But man, proud man,
Dressed in a little brief authority,
Most ignorant of what he's most assured,
His glassy essence, like an angry ape
Plays such fantastic tricks before high heaven
As makes the angels weep, who, with our spleens,
Would all themselves laugh mortal.

(Act 2, Scene 2)

DUKE
Be absolute for death. Either death or life
Shall thereby be the sweeter. Reason thus with life:
If I do lose thee, I do lose a thing
That none but fools would keep. A breath thou art,
Servile to all the skyey influences
That dost this habitation where thou keep'st
Hourly afflict. Merely thou art death's fool,
For him thou labour'st by thy flight to shun,
And yet run'st toward him still. Thou art not noble,
For all th'accommodations that thou bear'st
Are nursed by baseness. Thou'rt by no means valiant,
For thou dost fear the soft and tender fork
Of a poor worm. Thy best of rest is sleep,
And that thou oft provok'st, yet grossly fear'st
Thy death, which is no more. Thou art not thyself,
For thou exist'st on many a thousand grains
That issue out of dust. Happy thou art not,
For what thou hast not, still thou striv'st to get,
And what thou hast, forget'st. Thou art not certain,
For thy complexion shifts to strange effects
After the moon. If thou art rich, thou'rt poor,
For like an ass whose back with ingots bows,
Thou bear'st thy heavy riches but a journey,
And death unloads thee. Friend hast thou none,
For thine own bowels, which do call thee sire,
The mere effusion of thy proper loins,
Do curse the gout, serpigo, and the rheum
For ending thee no sooner. Thou hast nor youth nor age,
But as it were an after-dinner's sleep

Dreaming on both. For all thy blessèd youth
Becomes as agèd and doth beg the alms
Of palsied eld. And when thou art old and rich,
Thou hast neither heat, affection, limb, nor beauty
To make thy riches pleasant. What's in this
That bears the name of life? Yet in this life
Lie hid more thousand deaths. Yet death we fear
That makes these odds all even.

(Act 3, Scene 1)

CLAUDIO

Ay, but to die and go we know not where;
To lie in cold obstruction and to rot;
This sensible warm motion to become
A kneaded clod, and the delighted spirit
To bath in fiery floods or to recede
In thrilling region of thick-ribbed ice;
To be imprisoned in the viewless winds
And blown with restless violence round about
The pendant world; or to be worse than worst
Of those that lawless and incertain thought
Imagine howling—'tis too horrible.
The weariest and most loathèd worldly life
That age, ache, penury, and imprisonment
Can lay on nature is a paradise
To what we fear of death.

(Act 3, Scene 1)

SHYLOCK

He hath disgraced me and hindered me half a million, laughed at my losses, mocked at my gains, scorned my nation, thwarted my bargains, cooled my friends, heated mine enemies—and what's his reason? I am a Jew. Hath not a Jew eyes? Hath not a Jew hands, organs, dimensions, senses, affections, passions, fed with the same food, hurt with the same weapons, subject to the same diseases, healed by the same means, warmed and cooled by the same winter and summer as a Christian is? If you prick us do we not bleed? If you tickle us do we not laugh? If you poison us do we not die? And if you wrong us shall we not revenge? If we are like you in the rest, we will resemble you in that. If a Jew wrong a Christian, what is his humility? Revenge. If a Christian wrong a Jew, what should his sufferance be by Christian example? Why, revenge. The villainy you teach me I will execute, and it shall go hard but I will better the instruction.

(Act 3, Scene 1)

PORTIA

The quality of mercy is not strained.
It droppeth as the gentle rain from heaven
Upon the place beneath. It is twice blest:
It blesseth him that gives, and him that takes.
'Tis mightiest in the mightiest, it becomes
The thronèd monarch better than his crown.
His sceptre shows the force of temporal power,
The attribute to awe and majesty
Wherein doth sit the dread and fear of kings.
But mercy is above this sceptred sway.
It is enthronèd in the hearts of kings.
It is an attribute to God himself,
And earthly power doth then show likest God's
When mercy seasons justice.

(Act 4, Scene 1)

LORENZO

For do but note a wild and wanton herd
Or race of youthful and unhandled colts
Fetching mad bounds, bellowing and neighing loud,
Which is the hot condition of their blood,
If they but hear perchance a trumpet sound,
Or any air of music touch their ears,
You shall perceive them make a mutual stand,
Their savage eyes turned to a modest gaze
By the sweet power of music. Therefore the poet
Did fain that Orpheus drew trees, stones, and floods,
Since naught so stockish, hard, and full of rage
But music for the time doth change his nature.
The man that hath no music in himself,
Nor is not moved with concord of sweet sounds,
Is fit for treasons, stratagems, and spoils.
The motions of his spirit are dull as night,
And his affections dark as Erebus.
Let no such man be trusted. Mark the music.

(Act 5, Scene 1)

LYSANDER

The course of true love never did run smooth,
But either it was different in blood…
Or else misgrafted in respect of years…
Or else it stood upon the choice of friends…
Or if there were a sympathy in choice,
War, death, or sickness did lay siege to it,
Making it momentany as a sound,
Swift as a shadow, short as any dream,
Brief as the lightning in the collied night
That, in a spleen, unfolds both heaven and earth,
And ere a man hath power to say 'Behold!',
The jaws of darkness do devour it up.
So quick bright things come to confusion.

(Act 1, Scene 1)

TITANIA

The fairyland buys not the child of me.
His mother was a vot'ress of my order,
And in the spicèd Indian air by night
Full often hath she gossiped by my side,
And sat with me on Neptune's yellow sands
Marking th'embarkèd traders on the flood,
When we have laughed to see the sails conceive
And grow big-bellied with the wanton wind,
Which she with pretty and with swimming gait
Following, her womb then rich with my young squire,
Would imitate, and sail upon the land
To fetch me trifles, and return again,
As from a voyage, rich with merchandise.
But she, being mortal, of that boy did die.
And for her sake do I rear up her boy.
And for her sake I will not part with him.

(Act 2, Scene 1)

OBERON

Thou rememb'rest
Since once I sat upon a promontory
And heard a mermaid on a dolphin's back
Uttering such dulcet and harmonious breath
That the rude sea grew civil at her song,
And certain stars shot madly from their spheres
To hear the sea-maid's music?...
That very time I saw, but thou could'st not,
Flying between the cold moon and the earth,
Cupid all armed. A certain aim he took
At a fair vestal, thronèd by the west,
And loosed his love-shaft smartly from his bow
As it should pierce a hundred thousand hearts.
But I might see young Cupid's fiery shaft
Quenched in the chaste beams of the wat'ry moon,
And the imperial vot'ress passèd on
In maiden meditation, fancy-free.
Yet marked I where the bolt of Cupid fell.
It fell upon a little western flower,
Before, milk white, now purple with love's wound,
And maidens call it love-in-idleness.
Fetch me that flower, the herb I showed thee once.
The juice of it, on sleeping eyelids laid,
Will make or man or woman madly dote
Upon the next live creature that it sees.
Fetch me this herb.

(Act 2, Scene 1)

OBERON

I know a bank where the wild thyme blows,
Where oxlips and the nodding violet grows,
Quite overcanopied with luscious woodbine,
With sweet musk roses and with eglantine.
There sleeps Titania sometime of the night,
Lulled in these flowers with dances and delight.
And there the snake throws her enamelled skin,
Weed wide enough to wrap a fairy in.
And with the juice of this I'll streak her eyes
And make her full of hateful fantasies.

(Act 2, Scene 1)

BOTTOM

I have had a most rare vision. I have had a dream past the wit of man to say what dream it was. Man is but an ass if he go about to expound this dream. Methought I was—there is no man can tell what. Methought I was—and methought I had—but man is but a patched fool if he will offer to say what methought I had. The eye of man hath not heard, the ear of man hath not seen, man's hand is not able to taste, his tongue to conceive, nor his heart to report, what my dream was. I will get Peter Quince to write a balled of this dream. It shall be called 'Bottom's Dream', because it hath no bottom, and I will sing it in the latter end of a play, before the Duke. Peradventure, to make it the more gracious, I shall sing it at her death.

(Act 4, Scene 1)

THESEUS

Lovers and madmen have such seething brains,
Such shaping fantasies that apprehend
More than cool reason ever comprehends.
The lunatic, the lover, and the poet
Are of imagination all compact.
One sees more devils than vast hell can hold—
That is the madman. The lover, all as frantic,
Sees Helen's beauty in a brow of Egypt.
The poet's eye, in a fine frenzy rolling,
Doth glance from heaven to earth, from earth to heaven,
And as imagination bodies forth
The forms of things unknown, the poet's pen
Turns them to shapes and gives to airy nothing
A local habitation, and a name.
Such tricks hath strong imagination
That, if it would but apprehend some joy,
It comprehends some bringer of that joy.
Or, in the night, imagining some fear,
How easy is a bush supposed a bear?

(Act 5, Scene 1)

ROBIN

Now the hungry lion roars,
And the wolf behowls the moon,
Whilst the heavy ploughman snores
All with weary task fordone.
Now the wasted brands do glow,
Whilst the screech-owl, screeching loud,
Puts the wretch that lies in woe
In remembrance of a shroud.
Now it is the time of night
That the graves all gaping wide,
Every one lets forth his sprite
In the churchway paths to glide.
And we fairies, that do run
By the triple Hecate's team
From the presence of the sun
Following darkness like a dream,
Now are frolic. Not a mouse
Shall disturb this hallowed house.
I am sent with broom before
To sweep the dust behind the door.

(Act 5, Scene 2)

ROBIN

If we shadows have offended,
Think but this and all is mended:
That you have but slumbered here
While these visions did appear.
And this weak and idle theme,
No more yielding but a dream,
Gentles, do not reprehend.
If you pardon, we will mend.
And as I am an honest Puck,
If we have unearnèd luck,
Now to 'scape the serpent's tongue,
We will make amends ere long,
Else the Puck a liar call.
So, good night unto you all.
Give me your hands, if we be friends,
And Robin shall restore amends.

(Epilogue)

BALTHASAR

Sigh no more, ladies, sigh no more,
    Men were deceivers ever.
One foot in sea, and one on shore,
    To one thing constant never.
Then sigh not so, but let them go,
    And be you blithe and bonny,
Converting all your sounds of woe
    Into hey nonny, nonny.

Sing no more ditties, sing no more
    Of dumps so dull and heavy.
The fraud of men was ever so,
    Since summer first was leafy.
Then sigh not so, but let them go,
    And be you blithe and bonny,
Converting all your sounds of woe
    Into hey nonny, nonny.
                                (Act 2, Scene 3)

OTHELLO
Her father loved me, oft invited me,
Still questioned me the story of my life
From year to year, the battles, sieges, fortunes
That I have past.
I ran it through, even from my boyish days
To th'very moment that he bade me tell it,
Wherein I spoke of most disastrous chances,
Of moving accidents by flood and field,
Of hairbreadth scapes i'th' imminent deadly breach,
Of being taken by the insolent foe
And sold to slavery, of my redemption thence;
And portance in my traveller's history,
Wherein of antres vast and deserts idle,
Rough quarries, rocks, and hills whose heads touch heaven,
It was my hint to speak. Such was my process.
And of the cannibals that each other eat,
The Anthropophagi, and men whose heads
Do grow beneath their shoulders. These things to hear
Would Desdemona seriously incline.
But still the house affairs would draw her thence,
Which ever as she could with haste dispatch,
She'd come again, and with a greedy ear
Devour up my discourse. Which I observing,
Took once a pliant hour and found good means
To draw from her a prayer of earnest heart
That I would all my pilgrimage dilate,
Whereof by parcels she had something heard,
But not intentively. I did consent,
And often did beguile her of her tears

When I did speak of some distressful stroke
That my youth suffered. My story being done,
She gave me for my pains a world of sighs.
She swore in faith 'twas strange, 'twas passing strange,
'Twas pitiful, 'twas wondrous pitiful.
She wished she had not heard it, yet she wished
That heaven had made her such a man. She thanked me,
And bade me if I had a friend that loved her,
I should but teach him how to tell my story,
And that would woo her. Upon this hint I spake.
She loved me for the dangers I had past,
And I loved her that she did pity them.
This only is the witchcraft I have used.

(Act 1, Scene 3)

OTHELLO

I had been happy if the general camp,
Pioneers and all, had tasted her sweet body
So I had nothing known. O, now forever
Farewell the tranquil mind, farewell content,
Farewell the plumèd troops and the big wars
That makes ambition virtue! O, farewell,
Farewell the neighing steed and the shrill trump,
The spirit-stirring drum, th'ear-piercing fife,
The royal banner, and all quality,
Pride, pomp, and circumstance of glorious war!
And O, you mortal engines whose rude throats
Th'immortal Jove's dread clamours counterfeit,
Farewell! Othello's occupation's gone.

(Act 3, Scene 3)

OTHELLO
                    Had it pleased heaven
To try me with affliction, had they rained
All kind of sores and shames on my bare head,
Steeped me in poverty to the very lips,
Given to captivity me and my utmost hopes,
I should have found in some place of my soul
A drop of patience. But, alas, to make me
The fixèd figure for the time of scorn
To point his slow and moving finger at—
Yet could I bear that too, well, very well.
But there where I have garnered up my heart,
Where either I must live or bear no life,
The fountain from the which my current runs
Or else dries up—to be discarded thence,
Or keep it as a cistern for foul toads
To knot and gender in! Turn thy complexion there,
Patience, thou young and rose-lipped cherubin,
Ay, here look grim as hell.

                              (Act 4, Scene 2)

OTHELLO

It is the cause, it is the cause, my soul.
Let me not name it to you, you chaste stars.
It is the cause. Yet I'll not shed her blood,
Nor scar that whiter skin of hers than snow,
And smooth as monumental alabaster.
Yet she must die, else she'll betray more men.
Put out the light, and then put out the light.
If I quench thee, thou flaming minister,
I can again thy former light restore
Should I repent me. But once put out thy light,
Thou cunning'st pattern of excelling nature,
I know not where is that Promethean heat
That can thy light relume. When I have plucked thy rose,
I cannot give it vital growth again,
It needs must wither. I'll smell thee on the tree—
O balmy breath, that dost almost persuade
Justice to break her sword! One more, one more.
Be thus when thou art dead and I will kill thee
And love thee after. One more, and that's the last—
So sweet was ne'er so fatal. I must weep,
But they are cruel tears. This sorrow's heavenly,
It strikes where it doth love.

(Act 5, Scene 2)

OTHELLO

Soft you, a word or two before you go.
I have done the state some service, and they know't.
No more of that. I pray you, in your letters,
When you shall these unlucky deeds relate,
Speak of me as I am. Nothing extenuate,
Nor set down aught in malice. Then must you speak
Of one that loved not wisely, but too well;
Of one not easily jealous, but being wrought,
Perplexed in the extreme; of one whose hand,
Like the base Indian, threw a pearl away
Richer than all his tribe; of one whose subdued eyes,
Albeit unusèd to the melting mood,
Drops tears as fast as the Arabian trees
Their medicinable gum. Set you down this.
And say besides that in Aleppo once,
Where a malignant and a turbaned Turk
Beat a Venetian and traduced the state,
I took by th'throat the circumcisèd dog,
And smote him, thus.

(Act 5, Scene 2)

PERICLES
A terrible child-bed hast thou had, my dear.
No light, no fire. Th'unfriendly elements
Forgot thee utterly, nor have I time
To give thee hallowed to thy grave, but straight
Must cast thee, scarcely coffined, in the ooze,
Where for a monument upon thy bones
And aye-remaining lamps, the belching whale
And humming water must o'erwhelm thy corpse,
Lying with simple shells.

(Scene 11)

JOHN OF GAUNT

This royal throne of kings, this sceptred isle,
This earth of majesty, this seat of Mars,
This other Eden, demi-paradise,
This fortress built by nature for herself
Against infection and the hand of war,
This happy breed of men, this little world,
This precious stone set in the silver sea,
Which serves it in the office of a wall
Or as a moat defensive to a house
Against the envy of less happier lands,
This blessèd plot, this earth, this realm, this England,
This nurse, this teeming womb of royal kings
Feared by their breed and famous by their birth,
Renownèd for their deeds as far from home
For Christian service and true chivalry
As is the sepulchre in stubborn Jewry
Of the world's ransom, blessèd Mary's son,
This land of such dear souls, this dear, dear land,
Dear for her reputation through the world,
Is now leased out—I die pronouncing it—
Like to a tenement or pelting farm.
England, bound in with the triumphant sea,
Whose rocky shore beats back the envious siege
Of wat'ry Neptune, is now bound in with shame,
With inky blots and rotten parchment bonds.
That England that was wont to conquer others
Hath made a shameful conquest of itself.

(Act 2, Scene 1)

KING RICHARD

                    Of comfort no man speak.
Let's talk of graves, of worms and epitaphs,
Make dust our paper and with rainy eyes
Write sorrow on the bosom of the earth.
Let's choose executors and talk of wills.
And yet not so, for what can we bequeath,
Save our deposèd bodies, to the ground?
Our lands, our lives and all are Bolingbroke's.
And nothing can we call our own but death,
And that small model of the barren earth
Which serves as paste and cover to our bones.
For God's sake, let us sit upon the ground
And tell sad stories of the death of kings—
How some have been deposed, some slain in war,
Some haunted by the ghosts they have deposed,
Some poisoned by their wives, some sleeping killed,
All murdered. For within the hollow crown
That rounds the mortal temples of a king
Keeps death his court. And there the antic sits,
Scoffing his state and grinning at his pomp,
Allowing him a breath, a little scene,
To monarchize, be feared, and kill with looks,
Infusing him with self and vain conceit,
As if this flesh which walls about our life
Were brass impregnable. And humoured thus,
Comes at the last, and with a little pin
Bores through his castle wall, and farewell, king.
Cover your heads and mock not flesh and blood
With solemn reverence. Throw away respect,

Tradition, form, and ceremonious duty.
For you have but mistook me all this while.
I live with bread like you, feel want,
Taste grief, need friends. Subjected thus,
How can you say to me I am a king?

(Act 3, Scene 2)

KING RICHARD

What must the King do now? Must he submit?
The King shall do it. Must he be deposed?
The King shall be contented. Must he lose
The name of King? A God's name, let it go.
I'll give my jewels for a set of beads,
My gorgeous palace for a hermitage,
My gay apparel for an almsman's gown,
My figured goblets for a dish of wood,
My sceptre for a palmer's walking staff,
My subjects for a pair of carvèd saints,
And my large kingdom for a little grave,
A little, little grave, an obscure grave.
Or I'll be buried in the King's highway,
Some way of common trade, where subject's feet
May hourly trample on their sovereign's head,
For on my heart they tread now whilst I live,
And buried once, why not upon my head?
Aumerle, thou weep'st, my tender-hearted cousin.
We'll make foul weather with despisèd tears.
Our sighs and they shall lodge the summer corn,
And make a dearth in this revolting land.
Or shall we play the wantons with our woes,
And make some pretty match with shedding tears,
As thus to drop them still upon one place
Till they have fretted us a pair of graves
Within the earth, and therein laid? 'There lies
Two kinsmen digged their graves with weeping eyes.'
Would not this ill do well? Well, well, I see
I talk but idly and you mock at me.

Most mighty prince my Lord Northumberland,
What says King Bolingbroke? Will his majesty
Give Richard leave to live till Richard die?
You make a leg, and Bolingbroke says 'Ay'.

(Act 3, Scene 3)

KING RICHARD
Ay, no; no, ay. For I must nothing be.
Therefore no, no, for I resign to thee.
Now, mark me how I will undo myself:
I give this heavy weight from off my head,
And this unwieldy sceptre from my hand,
The pride of kingly sway from out my heart.
With mine own tears I wash away my balm,
With mine own hands I give away my crown,
With mine own tongue deny my sacred state,
With mine own breath release all duteous oaths.
All pomp and majesty I do forswear.
My manors, rents, revenues I forgo.
My acts, decrees, and statutes I deny.
God pardon all oaths that are broke to me.
God keep all vows unbroke are made to thee.
Make me, that nothing have, with nothing grieved,
And thou with all pleased, that hast all achieved.
Long may'st thou live in Richard's seat to sit,
And soon lie Richard in an earthy pit.
God save King Henry, unkinged Richard says,
And send him many years of sunshine days.
What more remains?

(Act 4, Scene 1)

KING RICHARD
I have been studying how I may compare
This prison where I live unto the world.
And for because the world is populous,
And here is not a creature but myself,
I cannot do it. Yet I'll hammer it out.
My brain I'll prove the female to my soul,
My soul the father, and these two beget
A generation of still-breeding thoughts,
And these same thoughts people this little world
In humours like the people of this world.
For no thought is contented. The better sort,
As thoughts of things divine, are intermixed
With scruples and do set the word itself
Against the word, as thus: 'Come, little ones.'
And then again:
'It is as hard to come as for a camel
To thread the postern of a small needle's eye.'
Thoughts tending to ambition, they do plot
Unlikely wonders: how these vain weak nails
May tear a passage through the flinty ribs
Of this hard world, my ragged prison walls,
And for they cannot, die in their own pride.
Thoughts tending to content flatter themselves
That they are not the first of fortune's slaves,
Nor shall not be the last, like seely beggars
Who, sitting in the stocks, refuge their shame
That many have, and others must, sit there.
And in this thought they find a kind of ease,
Bearing their own misfortunes on the back

Of such as have before endured the like.
Thus play I in one person many people,
And none contented. Sometimes am I king.
Then treasons make me wish myself a beggar,
And so I am. Then crushing penury
Persuades me I was better when a king.
Then am I kinged again, and by and by
Think that I am unkinged by Bolingbroke,
And straight am nothing. But whate'er I be,
Nor I nor any man that but man is,
With nothing shall be pleased till he be eased
With being nothing.

(Act 5, Scene 5)

RICHARD GLOUCESTER
Now is the winter of our discontent
Made glorious summer by this son of York,
And all the clouds that loured upon our house
In the deep bosom of the ocean buried.
Now are our brows bound with victorious wreathes,
Our bruisèd arms hung up for monuments,
Our stern alarums changed to merry meetings,
Our dreadful marches to delightful measures.
Grim-visaged war hath smoothed his wrinkled front,
And now, instead of mounting barbèd steeds
To fright the souls of fearful adversaries,
He capers nimbly in a lady's chamber
To the lascivious pleasing of a lute.
But I, that am not shaped for sportive tricks,
Nor made to court an amorous looking-glass,
I, that am rudely stamped, and want love's majesty
To strut before a wonton ambling nymph,
I, that am curtailed of this fair proportion,
Cheated of feature by dissembling nature,
Deformed, unfinished, sent before my time
Into this breathing world scarce half made up,
And that so lamely and unfashionable
That dogs bark at me as I halt by them,
Why, I, in this weak piping time of peace,
Have no delight to pass away the time
Unless to spy my shadow in the sun
And descant on mine own deformity.
And therefore, since I cannot prove a lover
To entertain these fair well-spoken days,

Richard III

I am determinèd to prove a villain,
And hate the idle pleasures of these days.

(Act 1 , Scene 1)

RICHARD GLOUCESTER
Was ever woman in this humour wooed?
Was ever woman in this humour won?
I'll have her, but I will not keep her long.
What, I that killed her husband and his father,
To take her in her heart's extremest hate,
With curses in her mouth, tears in her eyes,
The bleeding witness of my hatred by,
Having God, her conscience, and these bars against me,
And I, no friends to back my suit withal
But the plain devil and dissembling looks—
And yet to win her, all the world to nothing? Ha!
Hath she forgot already that brave prince,
Edward, her Lord, whom I, some three months since,
Stabbed in my angry mood at Tewkesbury?
A sweeter and a lovelier gentleman,
Framed in the prodigality of nature,
Young, valiant, wise, and, no doubt, right royal,
The spacious world cannot again afford.
And will she yet abase her eyes on me
That cropped the golden prime of this sweet prince
And made her widow to a woeful bed?
On me, whose all not equals Edward's moiety?
On me, that halts and am misshapen thus?
My dukedom to a beggarly *denier*,
I do mistake my person all this while.
Upon my life she finds, although I cannot,
Myself to be a marv'lous proper man.
I'll be at charges for a looking-glass,
And entertain a score or two of tailors

To study fashions to adorn my body.
Since I am crept in favour with myself
I will maintain it with some little cost.
But first I'll turn yon fellow in his grave
And then return lamenting to my love.
Shine out, fair sun, till I have bought a glass,
That I may see my shadow as I pass.

(Act 1, Scene 2)

CLARENCE

      Methought what pain it was to drown,
What dreadful noise of waters in mine ears,
What sights of ugly death within mine eyes.
Methoughts I saw a thousand fearful wrecks,
A thousand men that fishes gnawed upon,
Wedges of gold, great anchors, heaps of pearl,
Inestimable stones, unvalued jewels,
All scattered in the bottom of the sea.
Some lay in dead men's skulls, and in the holes
Where eyes did once inhabit there were crept,
As 'twere in scorn of eyes, reflecting gems
That wooed the slimy bottom of the deep,
And mocked the dead bones that lay scattered by.
                    (Act 1, Scene 4)

QUEEN MARGARET
I called thee then 'vain flourish of my fortune'.
I called thee then, poor shadow, 'painted queen',
The presentation of but what I was,
The flattering index of a direful pageant,
One heaved a-high to be hurled down below,
A mother only mocked with two fair babes,
A dream of what thou wast, a garish flag
To be the aim of every dangerous shot,
A sign of dignity, a breath, a bubble,
A queen in jest, only to fill the scene.
Where is thy husband now? Where be thy brothers?
Where be thy two sons? Wherein dost thou joy?
Who sues and kneels and says, 'God save the Queen'?
Where be the bending peers that flattered thee?
Where be the thronging troops that followed thee?
Decline all this, and see what now thou art:
For happy wife, a most distressèd widow;
For joyful mother, one that wails the name;
For one being sued to, one that humbly sues;
For queen, a very caitiff, crowned with care;
For she that scorned at me, now scorned of me;
For she being feared of all, now fearing one;
For she commanding all, obeyed of none.
Thus hath the course of justice whirled about
And left thee but a very prey to time,
Having no more but thought of what thou wast
To torture thee the more, being what thou art.
Thou didst usurp my place, and dost thou not
Usurp the just proportion of my sorrow?

Now thy proud neck bears half my burdened yoke
From which even here I slip my weary head
And leave the burden of it all on thee.
Farewell, York's wife, and queen of sad mischance.
These English woes shall make me smile in France.

(Act 4, Scene 4)

KING RICHARD
Give me another horse! Bind up my wounds!
Have mercy, Jesu!—Soft, I did but dream.
O coward conscience, how dost thou afflict me?
The lights burn blue. It is now dead midnight.
Cold fearful drops stand on my trembling flesh.
What do I fear? Myself? There's none else by.
Richard loves Richard, that is, I am I.
Is there a murderer here? No. Yes, I am.
Then fly. What, from myself? Great reason. Why?
Lest I revenge. What, myself upon myself?
Alack, I love myself. Wherefore? For any good
That I myself have done unto myself?
O no, alas, I rather hate myself
For hateful deeds committed by myself.
I am a villain. Yet I lie, I am not.
Fool, of thyself speak well. Fool, do not flatter.
My conscience hath a thousand several tongues,
And every tongue brings in a several tale,
And every tale condemns me for a villain.
Perjury, perjury in the highest degree,
Murder, stern murder, in the direst degree,
All several sins, all used in each degree,
Throng to the bar, crying all, 'Guilty! Guilty!'
I shall despair, there is no creature loves me.
And if I die no soul will pity me.
Nay, wherefore should they? Since that I myself
Find in myself no pity to myself.
Methought the souls of all that I had murdered

Came to my tent, and every one did threat
Tomorrow's vengeance on the head of Richard.

(Act 5, Scene 5)

CHORUS
Two households, both alike in dignity,
In fair Verona where we lay our scene,
From ancient grudge break to new mutiny,
Where civil blood makes civil hands unclean.
From forth the fatal loins of these two foes
A pair of star-crossed lovers take their life,
Whose misadventured piteous overthrows
Doth with their death bury their parents' strife.
The fearful passage of their death-marked love,
And the continuance of their parents' rage,
Which but their children's end naught could remove,
Is now the two-hours' traffic of our stage.
The which if you with patient ear attend,
What here shall miss, our toil shall strive to mend.

(Prologue)

NURSE
Even or odd, of all days in the year
Come Lammas Eve at night shall she be fourteen.
Susan and she—God rest all Christian souls!—
Were of an age. Well, Susan is with God,
She was too good for me. But as I said,
On Lammas Eve at night shall she be fourteen,
That shall she. Marry, I remember it well.
'Tis since the earthquake now eleven years.
And she was weaned, I never shall forget it,
Of all the days of the year upon that day.
For I had then laid wormwood to my dug,
Sitting in the sun under the dove house wall.
My Lord and you were then at Mantua—
Nay, I do bear a brain. But as I said,
When it did taste the wormwood on the nipple
Of my dug, and felt it bitter, pretty fool,
To see it tetchy and fall out with the dug.
'Shake', quoth the dove house! 'Twas no need, I trow,
To bid me trudge.
And since that time it is eleven years,
For then she could stand high-lone. Nay, by th'rood
She could have run and waddled all about.
For even the day before she broke her brow,
And then my husband—God be with his soul,
A was a merry man!—took up the child.
'Yea,' quoth he, 'dost thou fall upon thy face?
Thou wilt fall backward when thou hast more wit,
Wilt thou not, Jule?' And, by my halidom,
The pretty wretch left crying, and said 'Ay'.

To see now how a jest shall come about.
I warrant, an I should live a thousand years,
I never should forget it. 'Wilt thou not, Jule?' quoth he.
And, pretty fool, it stinted, and said 'Ay'...
             Yet I cannot choose but laugh
To think it should leave crying, and say 'Ay'.
And yet, I warrant it had upon it brow
A bump as big as a young cock'rel's stone,
A perilous knock, and it cried bitterly.
'Yea,' quoth my husband, 'fall'st upon thy face?
Thou wilt fall backward when thou comest to age,
Wilt thou not, Jule?' It stinted, and said 'Ay'.

(Act 1, Scene 3)

MERCUTIO
She is the fairies' midwife, and she comes
In shape no bigger than an agate stone
On the forefinger of an alderman,
Drawn with a team of little atomi,
Over men's noses as they lie asleep.
Her wagon spokes made of long spinners' legs;
The cover, of the wings of grasshoppers;
Her traces, of the smallest spider web;
Her collars, of the moonshines wat'ry beams;
Her whip, of cricket's bone, the lash of film;
Her wagoner, a small grey-coated gnat,
Not half so big as a round little worm,
Pricked from the lazy finger of a maid.
Her chariot is an empty hazelnut,
Made by the joiner squirrel or old grub,
Time out o' mind the fairies' coachmakers.
And in this state she gallops night by night
Through lovers brains, and then they dream of love;
O'er courtiers' knees, that dream on curtsies straight;
O'er lawyers fingers, who straight dream on fees;
O'er ladies' lips, who straight on kisses dream,
Which oft the angry Mab with blisters plagues
Because their breaths with sweetmeats tainted are.
Sometime she gallops o'er a courtier's nose,
And then dreams he of smelling out a suit.
And sometime comes she with a tithe-pig's tail,
Tickling a person's nose as a lies asleep,
Then dreams he of another benefice.
Sometime she driveth o'er a soldier's neck,

And then dreams he of cutting foreign throats,
Of breaches, ambuscados, Spanish blades,
Of healths five fathom deep, and then anon
Drums in his ear, at which he starts and wakes
And being thus frighted swears a prayer or two,
And sleeps again. This is that very Mab
That plaits the manes of horses in the night,
And bakes the elf-locks in foul sluttish hairs,
Which once untangled, much misfortune bodes.
This is the hag, when maids lie on their backs,
That presses them and learns them first to bear,
Making them women of good carriage—
This is she.

(Act 1, Scene 4)

138

ROMEO

O, she doth teach the torches to burn bright!
It seems she hangs upon the cheek of night
As a rich jewel in an Ethiope's ear,
Beauty too rich for use, for earth too dear.
So shows a snowy dove trooping with crows
As yonder lady o'er her fellows shows.
The measure done, I'll watch her place of stand,
And touching hers make blessed my rude hand.
Did my heart love till now? Forswear it, sight,
For I ne'er saw true beauty till this night.

(Act 1, Scene 5)

ROMEO AND JULIET
If I profane with my unworthiest hand
   This holy shrine, the gentle sin is this:
My lips two blushing pilgrims ready stand
   To smooth that rough touch with a tender kiss.
Good pilgrim, you do wrong your hand too much,
   Which mannerly devotion shows in this.
For saints have hands that pilgrims' hands do touch,
   And palm to palm is holy palmers' kiss.
Have not saints lips and holy palmers too?
   Ay, pilgrim, lips that they must use in prayer.
O then, dear saint, let lips do what hands do:
   They pray, grant thou, lest faith turn to despair.
Saints do not move, though grant for prayers' sake.
Then move not while my prayer's effect I take—

Thus from my lips by thine my sin is purged.
   Then have my lips the sin that they have took.
Sin from my lips? O, trespass sweetly urged!
   Give me my sin again—*You kiss by th'book.*
                     (Act 1, Scene 5)

ROMEO

But soft, what light through yonder window breaks?
It is the east, and Juliet is the sun.
Arise fair sun and kill the envious moon,
Who is already sick and pale with grief
That thou her maid art far more fair than she.
Be not her maid, since she is envious.
Her vestal livery is but sick and green,
And none but fools do wear it. Cast it off.
It is my lady, O, it is my love!
O, that she knew she were.
She speaks, yet she says nothing, what of that?
Her eye discourses, I will answer it—
I am too bold, 'tis not to me she speaks.
Two of the fairest stars in all the heaven,
Having some business, do entreat her eyes
To twinkle in their spheres till they return.
What if her eyes were there, they in her head?
The brightness of her cheek would shame those stars
As daylight doth a lamp. Her eye in heaven
Would through the airy region stream so bright
That birds would sing and think it were not night.
See how she leans her cheek upon her hand.
O, that I were a glove upon that hand,
That I might touch that cheek…She speaks!
O, speak again bright angel, for thou art
As glorious to this night being o'er my head,
As is a wingèd messenger of heaven
Unto the white upturnèd wond'ring eyes
Of mortals that fall back to gaze on him

When he bestrides the lazy puffing clouds
And sails upon the bosom of the air.

(Act 2, Scene 1)

JULIET

O Romeo, Romeo, wherefore art thou Romeo?
Deny thy father and refuse thy name.
Or if thou wilt not, be but sworn my love,
And I'll no longer be a Capulet...
'Tis but thy name that is my enemy.
Thou art thyself, though not a Montague.
What's Montague? It is nor hand, nor foot,
Nor arm, nor face, nor any other part
Belonging to a man. O, be some other name!
What's in a name? That which we call a rose
By any other word would smell as sweet.
So Romeo would, were he not Romeo called,
Retain that dear perfection which he owes
Without that title. Romeo, doff thy name,
And for thy name, which is no part of thee,
Take all myself.

(Act 2, Scene 1)

JULIET

Gallop apace, you fiery-footed steeds,
Towards Phoebus' lodging! Such a wagoner
As Phaeton would whip you to the west
And bring in cloudy night immediately.
Spread thy close curtain, love-performing night,
That runaways' eyes may wink, and Romeo
Leap to these arms untalked of and unseen.
Lovers can see to do their amorous rites
By their own beauties, or if love be blind,
It best agrees with night. Come, civil night,
Thou sober-suited matron all in black,
And learn me how to lose a winning match
Played for a pair of stainless maidenhoods.
Hood my unmanned blood, bating in my cheeks,
With thy black mantle till strange love grow bold,
Think true love acted simple modesty.
Come night, come Romeo, come thou day in night!
For thou wilt lie upon the wings of night
Whiter than new snow upon a raven's back.
Come, gentle night, come, loving black-browed night,
Give me my Romeo, and when I shall die
Take him and cut him out in little stars,
And he will make the face of heaven so fine
That all the world will be in love with night
And pay no worship to the garish sun.
O, I have bought the mansion of a love
But not possessed it, and though I am sold,
Not yet enjoyed. So tedious is this day
As is the night before some festival

To an impatient child that hath new robes
And may not wear them.

(Act 3, Scene 2)

MORE

Grant them removed, and grant that this your noise
Hath chid down all the majesty of England.
Imagine that you see the wretched strangers,
Their babies at their backs, and their poor luggage,
Plodding to th'ports and coasts for transportation,
And that you sit as kings in your desires,
Authority quite silent by your brawl,
And you in ruff of your opinions clothed.
What had you got? I'll tell you. You had taught
How insolence and strong hand should prevail,
How order should be quelled, and by this pattern
Not one of you should live an agèd man,
For other ruffians, as their fancies wrought
With selfsame hand, self reasons, and self right,
Would shark on you, and men like ravenous fishes
Would feed on one another.

(Add.II.D)

ARIEL AND SPIRITS
Come unto these yellow sands,
    and then take hands.
Curtsied when you have, and kissed
    the wild waves whist.
Foot it featly here and there, and sweet sprites bear
    the burden.

Hark, hark! Bow-wow! The watch-dogs bark,
    bow-wow.

Hark, hark, I hear the strain of strutting chanticleer
    cry cock-a-diddle-dow.

(Act 1, Scene 2)

ARIEL
Full fathom five thy father lies.
Of his bones are coral made,
Those are pearls that were his eyes,
Nothing of him that doth fade
But doth suffer a sea-change
Into something rich and strange.
Sea nymphs hourly ring his knell.
Hark, now I hear them, ding-dong bell.
                    (Act 1, Scene 2)

CALIBAN
Be not afeard. The isle is full of noises,
Sounds and sweet airs that give delight and hurt not.
Sometimes a thousand twangling instruments
Will hum about mine ears, and sometimes voices,
That if I then had waked after long sleep
Will make me sleep again, and then in dreaming
The clouds methought would open and show riches
Ready to drop upon me, that when I waked
I cried to dream again.

(Act 3, Scene 2)

PROSPERO

Our revels now are ended. These our actors,
As I foretold you, were all spirits and
Are melted into air, into thin air.
And like the baseless fabric of this vision,
The cloud-capped towers, the gorgeous palaces,
The solemn temples, the great globe itself,
Yea, all which it inherit, shall dissolve,
And like this insubstantial pageant faded,
Leave not a rack behind. We are such stuff
As dreams are made on, and our little life
Is rounded with a sleep.

(Act 4, Scene 1)

PROSPERO

Ye elves of hills, brooks, standing lakes, and groves,
And ye that on the sands with printless foot
Do chase the ebbing Neptune, and do fly him
When he comes back; you demi-puppets that
By moonshine do the green sour ringlets make
Whereof the ewe not bites; and you whose pastime
Is to make midnight mushrooms, that rejoice
To hear the solemn curfew; by whose aid,
Weak masters though ye be, I have bedimmed
The noontide sun, called forth the mutinous winds,
And 'twixt the green sea and the azured vault
Set roaring war; to the dread rattling thunder
Have I given fire, and rifted Jove's stout oak
With his own bolt; the strong-based promontory
Have I made shake, and by the spurs plucked up
The pine and cedar; graves at my command
Have waked their sleepers, op'd, and let 'em forth
By my so potent art. But this rough magic
I here abjure. And, when I have required
Some heavenly music, which even now I do,
To work mine end upon their senses that
This airy charm is for, I'll break my staff,
Bury it certain fathoms in the earth,
And deeper than did ever plummet sound
I'll drown my book.

(Act 5, Scene 1)

PROSPERO

Now my charms are all o'erthrown,
And what strength I have's mine own,
Which is most faint. Now 'tis true
I must be here confined by you,
Or sent to Naples. Let me not,
Since I have my dukedom got
And pardoned the deceiver, dwell
In this bare island by your spell,
But release me from my bands
With the help of your good hands.
Gentle breath of yours my sails
Must fill, or else my project fails,
Which was to please. Now I want
Spirits to enforce, art to enchant,
And my ending is despair
Unless I be relieved by prayer,
Which pierces so, that it assaults
Mercy itself, and frees all faults.
    As you from crimes would pardoned be,
    Let your indulgence set me free.

(Epilogue)

APEMANTUS

Immortal gods, I crave no pelf.
I pray for no man but myself.
Grant I may never prove so fond
To trust man on his oath or bond,
Or a harlot for her weeping,
Or a dog that seems asleeping,
Or a keeper with my freedom,
Or my friends if I should need 'em.
Amen.

(Act 1, Scene 2)

TIMON

Let me look back upon thee. O thou wall
That girdles in those wolves, dive in the earth
And fence not Athens! Matrons, turn incontinent!
Obedience fail in children! Slaves and fools,
Pluck the grave wrinkled senate from the bench
And minister in their steads! To general filths
Convert o'th' instant green virginity!
Do't in your parents' eyes. Bankrupts, hold fast!
Rather than render back, out with your knives
And cut your trusters' throats! Bound servants, steal!
Large-handed robbers your grave masters are,
And pill by law. Maid, to thy master's bed!
Thy mistress is o'th' brothel. Son of sixteen,
Pluck the lined crutch from thy old limping sire,
With it beat out his brains! Piety and fear,
Religion to the gods, peace, justice, truth,
Domestic awe, night-rest, and neighbourhood,
Instruction, manners, mysteries, and trades,
Degrees, observances, customs, and laws,
Decline to your confounding contraries,
And let confusion live! Plagues incident to men,
Your potent and infectious fevers heap
On Athens ripe for stroke! Thou cold sciatica,
Cripple our senators, that their limbs may halt
As lamely as their manners! Lust and liberty,
Creep in the minds and marrows of our youth,
That 'gainst the stream of virtue they may strive
And drown themselves in riot! Itches, blains,
Sow all th'Athenian bosoms, and their crop

Be general leprosy! Breath infect breath,
That their society, as their friendship, may
Be merely poison! Nothing I'll bear from thee
But nakedness, thou detestable town.
Take thou that too, with multiplying bans.
Timon will to the woods where he shall find
Th'unkindest beast more kinder than mankind.
The gods confound—hear me you good gods all—
Th'Athenians both within and out that wall.
And grant, as Timon grows, his hate may grow
To the whole race of mankind, high and low.
Amen.

(Act 4, Scene 1)

TIMON

                             Hold up, you sluts,
Your aprons mountant. You are not oathable,
Although I know you'll swear, terribly swear,
Into strong shudders and to heavenly agues
Th'immortal gods that hear you. Spare your oaths.
I'll trust to your conditions. Be whores still,
And he whose pious breath seeks to convert you,
Be strong in whore, allure him, burn him up,
Let your close fire predominate his smoke,
And be no turncoats. Yet may your pain-sick months
Be quite contrary. And thatch
Your poor thin roofs with burdens of the dead—
Some that were hanged, no matter.
Wear them, betray with them. Whore still.
Paint till a horse may mire upon your face.
A pox of wrinkles!

                                       (Act 4, Scene 3)

TIMON

                        Rascal thieves,
Here's gold. Go suck the subtle blood o'th' grape
Till the high fever seethe your blood to froth,
And so 'scape hanging. Trust not the physician,
His antidotes are poison, and he slays
More than you rob. Take wealth and lives together.
Do villainy, do, since you protest to do't,
Like workmen. I'll example you with thievery:
The sun's a thief, and with his great attraction
Robs the vast sea. The moon's an arrant thief,
And her pale fire she snatches from the sun.
The sea's a thief, whose liquid surge resolves
The moon into salt tears. The earth's a thief,
That feeds and breeds by a composture stol'n
From general excrement. Each thing's a thief.
The laws, your curb and whip, in their rough power
Has unchecked theft. Love not yourselves. Away,
Rob one another. There's more gold. Cut throats,
All that you meet are thieves. To Athens go,
Break open shops. Nothing can you steal
But thieves do lose it. Steal no less for this I give you,
And gold confound you howsoe'er. Amen.
(Act 4, Scene 3)

TIMON
Come not to me again, but say to Athens
Timon hath made his everlasting mansion
Upon the beachèd verge of the salt flood,
Who once a day with his embossèd froth
The turbulent surge shall cover. Thither come,
And let my gravestone be your oracle.
Lips, let four words go by, and language end.
What is amiss, plague and infection mend.
Graves only be men's works, and death their gain.
Sun, hide thy beams, Timon hath done his reign.

(Act 5, Scene 2)

AARON

Ay, that I had not done a thousand more.
Even now I curse the day, and yet I think
Few come within the compass of my curse,
Wherein I did not some notorious ill,
As kill a man or else devise his death,
Ravish a maid or plot the way to do it,
Accuse some innocent and forswear myself,
Set deadly enmity between two friends,
Make poor men's cattle break their necks,
Set fire on barns and haystacks in the night
And bid the owners quench them with their tears.
Oft have I digged up dead men from their graves
And set them upright at their dear friends' door,
Even when their sorrows almost was forgot,
And on their skins as on the bark of trees
Have with my knife carved in Roman letters,
'Let not your sorrow die though I am dead.'
But I have done a thousand dreadful things
As willingly as one would kill a fly,
And nothing grieves me heartily indeed
But that I cannot do ten thousand more.

(Act 5, Scene 1)

CRESSIDA
Words, vows, gifts, tears, and love's full sacrifice
He offers in another's enterprise.
But more in Troilus thousandfold I see
Than in the glass of Pandar's praise may be.
Yet hold I off. Women are angels, wooing;
Things won are done, joy's soul lies in the doing.
That she beloved knows naught that knows not this:
Men prize the thing ungained more than it is.
That she was never yet that ever knew
Love got so sweet as when desire did sue.
Therefore this maxim out of love I teach:
Achievement is command; ungained, beseech.
Then, though my heart's contents firm love doth bear,
Nothing of that shall from mine eyes appear.

(Act 1, Scene 2)

ULYSSES
The specialty of rule hath been neglected,
And look how many Grecian tents do stand
Hollow upon this plain, so many hollow factions.
When that the general is not like the hive,
To whom the foragers shall all repair,
What honey is expected? Degree being vizarded,
Th'unworthiest shows as fairly in the mask.
The heavens themselves, the planets and this centre,
Observe degree, priority, and place,
Insisture, course, proportion, season, form,
Office, and custom in all line of order.
And therefore is the glorious planet Sol
In noble eminence enthroned and sphered
Amidst the other, whose med'cinable eye
Corrects the ill aspects of planets evil,
And posts like the commandment of a king,
Sans check, to good and bad. But when the planets
In evil mixture to disorder wander,
What plagues and what portents, what mutiny?
What raging of the sea, shaking of earth,
Commotion in the winds, frights, changes, horrors
Divert and crack, rend and deracinate
The unity and married calm of states
Quite from their fixture? O, when degree is shaked,
Which is the ladder to all high designs,
The enterprise is sick. How could communities,
Degrees in schools and brotherhoods in cities,
Peaceful commerce from dividable shores,
The primogenitive and due of birth,

Prerogative of age, crowns, sceptres, laurels,
But by degree stand in authentic place?
Take but degree away, untune that string,
And hark what discord follows. Each thing meets
In mere oppugnancy. The bounded waters
Should lift their bosoms higher than the shores
And make a sop of all this solid globe.
Strength should be lord of imbecility,
And the rude son should strike his father dead.
Force should be right—or rather, right and wrong,
Between whose endless jar justice resides,
Should lose their names, and so should justice too.
Then everything includes itself in power,
Power into will, will into appetite,
And appetite, an universal wolf,
So doubly seconded with will and power,
Must make perforce an universal prey,
And last eat up himself. Great Agamemnon,
This chaos, when degree is suffocate,
Follows the choking.
And this neglection of degree it is
That by a pace goes backward in a purpose
It hath to climb: the general's disdained
By him one step below; he, by the next;
That next by him beneath—so every step,
Exampled by the first pace that is sick
Of his superior, grows to an envious fever
Of pale and bloodless emulation.
And 'tis this fever that keeps Troy on foot,

Not her own sinews. To end a tale of length,
Troy in our weakness lives, not in her strength.

(Act 1, Scene 3)

TROILUS
I am giddy. Expectation whirls me round.
Th'imaginary relish is so sweet
That it enchants my sense. What will it be
When that the wat'ry palates taste indeed
Love's thrice-repurèd nectar? Death, I fear me,
Sounding destruction, or some joy too fine,
Too subtle-potent, tuned too sharp in sweetness
For the capacity of my ruder powers.
I fear it much, and I do fear besides
That I shall lose distinction in my joys,
As doth a battle when they charge on heaps
The enemy flying.

(Act 3, Scene 2)

ULYSSES

Time hath, my Lord,
A wallet at his back, wherein he puts
Alms for oblivion, a great-sized monster
Of ingratitudes. Those scraps are good deeds past,
Which are devoured as fast as they are made,
Forgot as soon as done. Perseverance, dear my Lord,
Keeps honour bright. To have done is to hang
Quite out of fashion, like a rusty mail
In monumental mock'ry. Take the instant way,
For honour travels in a strait so narrow
Where one but goes abreast. Keep then the path,
For emulation hath a thousand sons
That one by one pursue. If you give way
Or hedge aside from the direct forthright,
Like to an entered tide they all rush by
And leave you hindmost.
Or, like a gallant horse fall'n in first rank,
Lie there for pavement to the abject rear,
O'errun and trampled on. Then what they do in present,
Though less than yours in past, must o'ertop yours.
For Time is like a fashionable host
That slightly shakes his parting guest by th'hand,
And, with his arms outstretched as he would fly,
Grasps in the comer. Welcome ever smiles,
And Farewell goes out sighing. O, let not virtue seek
Remuneration for the thing it was.
For beauty, wit,
High birth, vigour of bone, desert in service,
Love, friendship, charity, are subjects all

To envious and calumniating Time.
One touch of nature makes the whole world kin,
That all with one consent praise new-born gauds,
Though they are made and moulded of things past,
And give to dust that is a little gilt
More laud than gilt o'erdusted.
The present eye praises the present object.

(Act 3, Scene 3)

TROILUS

And suddenly, where injury of chance
Puts back leave-taking, jostles roughly by
All time of pause, rudely beguiles our lips
Of all rejoindure, forcibly prevents
Our locked embrasures, strangles our dear vows
Even in the birth of our own labouring breath.
We two, that with so many thousand sighs
Did buy each other, must poorly sell ourselves
With the rude brevity and discharge of one.
Injurious Time now with a robber's haste
Crams his rich thiev'ry up, he know not how.
As many farewells as be stars in heaven,
With distinct breath and consigned kisses to them,
He fumbles up into a loose adieu
And scants us with a single famished kiss,
Distasted with the salt of broken tears.

(Act 4, Scene 5)

ORSINO

If music be the food of love, play on.
Give me excess of it that, surfeiting,
The appetite may sicken and so die.
That strain again, it had a dying fall.
O, it came o'er my ear like the sweet sound
That breathes upon a bank of violets,
Stealing and giving odour. Enough, no more,
'Tis not so sweet now as it was before.
O spirit of love, how quick and fresh art thou
That, notwithstanding thy capacity
Receiveth as the sea, naught enters there,
Of what validity and pitch so e'er,
But falls into abatement and low price
Even in a minute. So full of shapes is fancy
That it alone is high fantastical.

(Act 1, Scene 1)

VIOLA

Make me a willow cabin at your gate,
And call upon my soul within the house;
Write loyal cantons of contemnèd love,
And sing them loud even in the dead of night;
Hallow your name to the reverberate hills,
And make the babbling gossip of the air
Cry out 'Olivia!' O, you should not rest
Between the elements of air and earth,
But you should pity me.

(Act 1, Scene 5)

FESTE

O mistress mine, where are you roaming?
O, stay and hear, your true love's coming,
   That can sing both high and low.
Trip no further, pretty sweeting,
Journeys end in lover's meeting,
   Every wise man's son doth know.

What is love? 'Tis not hereafter,
Present mirth hath present laughter,
   What's to come is still unsure.
In delay there lies no plenty,
Then come kiss me sweet and twenty,
   Youth's a stuff will not endure.

(Act 2, Scene 3)

FESTE

Come away, come away death,
And in sad cypress let me be laid.
Fie away, fie away breath,
I am slain by a fair cruel maid.
  My shroud of white, stuck all with yew, O prepare it.
  My part of death no one so true did share it.

Not a flower, not a flower sweet
On my black coffin let there be strewn.
Not a friend, not a friend greet
My poor corpse, where my bones shall be thrown.
  A thousand thousand sighs to save, lay me O where
  Sad true lover never find my grave, to weep there.
                                          (Act 2, Scene 4)

FESTE

When that I was and a little tiny boy,
   with hey, ho, the wind and the rain,
A foolish thing was but a toy,
   for the rain it raineth every day.

But when I came to man's estate,
   with hey, ho, the wind and the rain,
'Gainst knaves and thieves men shut their gate,
   for the rain it raineth every day.

But when I came, alas, to wive,
   with hey, ho, the wind and the rain,
By swaggering could I never thrive,
   for the rain it raineth every day.

But when I came unto my beds,
   with hey, ho, the wind and the rain,
With tosspots still had drunken heads,
   for the rain it raineth every day.

A great while ago the world begun,
   with hey, ho, the wind and the rain,
But that's all one, our play is done,
   and we'll strive to please you every day.
                   (Act 5, Scene 1)

LEONTES

Inch-thick, knee-deep, o'er head and ears a forked one.
Go play, boy, play. Thy mother plays, and I
Play too, but so disgraced a part, whose issue
Will hiss me to my grave. Contempt and clamour
Will be my knell. Go play, boy, play. There have been,
Or I am much deceived, cuckolds ere now,
And many a man there is, even at this present,
Now, while I speak this, holds his wife by th'arm,
That little thinks she has been sluiced in's absence,
And his pond fished by his next neighbour, by
Sir Smile, his neighbour. Nay, there's comfort in't,
Whiles other men have gates, and those gates opened,
As mine, against their will. Should all despair
That have revolted wives, the tenth of mankind
Would hang themselves. Physic for't there's none.
It is a bawdy planet, that will strike
Where 'tis predominant. And 'tis powerful, think it,
From east, west, north, and south, be it concluded,
No barricado for a belly. Know't,
It will let in and out the enemy
With bag and baggage. Many thousand on's
Have the disease and feel't not.

(Act 1, Scene 2)

LEONTES

                              Is whispering nothing?
Is leaning cheek to cheek? Is meeting noses?
Kissing with inside lip? Stopping the career
Of laughter with a sigh, a note infallible
Of breaking honesty? Horsing foot on foot?
Skulking in corners? Wishing clocks more swift?
Hours, minutes? Noon, midnight? And all eyes
Blind with the pin and web but theirs, theirs only,
That would unseen be wicked? Is this nothing?
Why then the world and all that's in't is nothing,
The covering sky is nothing, Bohemia nothing,
My wife is nothing, nor nothing have these nothings
If this be nothing.

                                      (Act 1, Scene 2)

LEONTES

      There may be in the cup
A spider steeped, and one may drink, depart,
And yet partake no venom, for his knowledge
Is not infected. But if one present
Th'abhorred ingredient to his eye, make known
How he hath drunk, he cracks his gorge, his sides,
With violent hefts. I have drunk, and seen the spider.
           (Act 2, Scene 1)

FLORIZEL

What you do
Still betters what is done. When you speak, sweet,
I'd have you do it ever. When you sing,
I'd have you buy and sell so, so give alms,
Pray so, and for the ord'ring your affairs,
To sing them too. When you do dance, I wish you
A wave o'th' sea, that you might ever do
Nothing but that, move still, still so,
And own no other function. Each your doing,
So singular in each particular,
Crowns what you are doing in the present deeds,
That all your acts are queens.

(Act 4, Scene 4)

INDEX OF FIRST LINES

CPSIA information can be obtained at www.ICGtesting.com
Printed in the USA
LVOW10s1552170815

450441LV00005B/562/P